CONTENTS

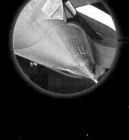
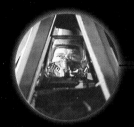

Xplanes

Since the dawn of aviation, designers have always worked on 'secret' projects — trying to build a experimental flying machine that was more advanced than any other. This was especially important during wartime, and it was Germany's ultra-secret World War Two projects that elevated the race for technological superiority to new heights.

The Germans were the first to use codenames to hide the identity of numerous secret experimental programmes, many of which were technically far in advance of those being developed at the time by the Allies — the V-1 and Me-262 were just two examples. This inspired the United States to form top-security units of highly-qualified designers and technicians to work on advanced experimental aircraft programmes that led directly to the establishment of Lockheed's famous Skunk Works.

However, it was the Cold War that gave birth to the 'black' aircraft programme in the USA — when billions of dollars were covertly spent on aircraft, with very few members of the government even aware of their existence.

Many of these projects proved to be spectacular leaps forward in technology and military capability, thus justifying their enormous cost. The old adage of 'information is power' was emphasised by the fact that many of the most successful US 'black' projects were covert reconnaissance aircraft — the high-flying U-2, the Mach 3 SR-71 and the latest generation of unmanned reconnaissance aerial vehicles (URAV) such as DarkStar.

The 'enemy' during the Cold War, the Soviet Union was well aware that it was losing the surveillance battle, not because its designers were any less capable than the Americans, but because few had the wholehearted support of the Politburo and consequently many revolutionary concepts never progressed beyond the drawing board.

Britain and France were never major players in 'black' technology although they have belatedly begun to co-operate in the possible development of future advanced air systems — the only 'enemy' now being the ever more powerful US aerospace industry which is still capable of investing huge amounts of money in military programmes, both openly and covertly.

The following chapters detail Lockheed's Skunk Works and McDonnell Douglas' Phantom Works, profile the development and operational lives of former 'black' projects such as the U-2, SR-71, F-117A and B-2A, look at the Soviet Union's 'black' projects and reveal some of futuristic designs of combat air systems of the next century.   Welcome to X-planes!

SKUNK WORKS

WHEN CLARENCE L 'Kelly' Johnson brought together a hand-picked team of Lockheed engineers and manufacturing personnel in 1943, each team member was cautioned that the design and production of a new jet fighter must be carried out in strict secrecy. No one was to discuss the project outside that small organisation and team members were even warned to be careful how they answered the telephone.

This was the second year of the United States' involvement in World War Two and the secret aircraft that Lockheed was working on was the XP-80, later to be christened the Shooting Star.

One of the team engineers, named Irven Culver, was a keen fan of Al Capp's famous newspaper comic strip, 'Li'l Abner' in which there was a running joke about a mysterious place deep in the forest called the 'Skonk Works'. There, a strange beverage was brewed from skunks, old shoes and other assorted ingredients. One day Culver's

phone rang and he answered it by saying "Skonk Works, inside man Culver speaking." Fellow employees in the team quickly adopted the name for their mysterious department where the new jet fighter project was materialising. Later 'Skonk Works' became 'Skunk Works' and the once informal nickname of a high-security operation was registered

Lockheed's secret aerospace plants, known collectively as the Skunk Works, produced some of the most successful special purpose aircraft in history.

Gate 3
Prohibited
Weapons, Explosives, Illegal Drugs, Alcohol, Cameras, Film, Computers, Electronic and Recording Devices

Vehicles Subject to Search Rules and Regulations Strictly Enforced

Above: The Skunk Works' headquarters at Palmdale. (Rick Spurway)

Left: The first aircraft built by the Skunk Works at Burbank was the XP-60, seen here at Muroc Army Air Field in 1944. (Lockheed)

as a trademark of the company, thereafter known as Lockheed Martin Skunk Works.

Before then, new projects were designed and developed by the Lockheed Advanced Aeronautics Company, later the Lockheed Advanced Development Company (LADC), which had its headquarters at Burbank. This is where the first Shooting Star prototype, the XP-80, was built before being transported to Muroc Army Air Field for its first flight on January 8, 1944.

Other products of the Burbank Skunk Works were the F-94 Starfire, the XF-90 and the XFV-1 vertical take-off and landing turboprop-powered fighter. By 1953, Kelly Johnson had become Lockheed's chief engineer and was soon presiding over the move to a new custom-built 'Skunk Works' at a remote location at Palmdale Airport, California, 35 miles (56km) north of Burbank.

While this was taking place, another advanced fighter project was taking shape at Burbank designed by Kelly Johnson's team. It was the supersonic XF-104 which was later trucked to Edwards AFB for its first flight. The aircraft made its first flight on March 4, 1954, with Tony LeVier at the controls. Despite limited sales to the USAF, more than 2,500 F-104 Starfighters were subsequently built, most of which were manufactured in Europe, Canada and Japan.

A Skunk Works milestone, not just for the extreme secrecy which surrounded the project, but because design, development and all production aircraft were built by Kelly Johnson's team, was Project *Aquatone*, better known to the rest of the world as the U-2.

Although the prototype of the high-altitude reconnaissance aircraft was assembled at Burbank and flown to Area 51 in Nevada for its first flight on August 4, 1955, with Tony LeVier again at the controls, most of the production U-2As were built at a satellite plant at Oildale near Bakersfield, 90 miles (145km) north of Burbank.

The first U-2s were operated by the CIA for covert flights over the Soviet Union, but these came to an abrupt end with the shooting down of the U-2 piloted by Gary Powers on May Day 1960.

This event prompted the design of a new high-performance reconnaissance aircraft that could outrun any known Soviet fighter aircraft or surface-to-air missiles

(SAM). The outcome of these studies was another success for Kelly Johnson and his Skunk Works. No less than three projects, *Senior Bowl, Tagboard* and *Senior Crown,* (profiled in detail in later chapters) kept the United States way ahead of the Soviet Union in both performance and technology. Although the A-12 had a short operational life span and the D-21 drone never reached its full potential, the SR-71 more than lived up to the Skunk Works' expectations. It was a brilliantly successful high-performance reconnaissance platform, it covered conflicts in South East Asia and the Middle East, flew surveillance flights over Cuba and Nicaragua and observed the Soviet Union from on high. Over a period of 25 years, both the Mach 3 A-12 and the SR-71 were to establish numerous absolute height and speed records, many of which remain unbroken to this day. All production of the A-12/SR-71 aircraft was based at Burbank.

In 1972, Ben Rich was appointed President of Advanced Development Projects (APD) paving the way for Kelly Johnson's retirement in 1975, although he was retained as a senior advisor. He died in 1990.

Ben Rich joined Lockheed in 1950 as an engineer working on all aspects of the F-104, U-2, YF-12 and SR-71 programmes before becoming senior engineer for advanced programmes in 1963. He officially retired in 1991, but like Kelly Johnson before him, he was retained by Lockheed as a senior advisor.

Throughout the 1960s and '70s, the height of the *Cold War* with the Soviet Union, the Skunk Works' main preoccupation was with reconnaissance aircraft. However Lockheed's advanced lightweight fighter project, the X-27 Lancer was one of the department's few failures. Launched in 1971 as a private venture and aimed at the USAF in competition with General Dynamics' F-16, and later as a replacement for NATO's F-104G, the Lancer project was cancelled in August 1973 due to lack of interest.

The cancellation of the X-27 left a void at the Skunk Works in the mid-1970s. Apart from upgrades to the U-2 and SR-71, production at Palmdale had virtually ground to a halt.

The Lockheed, company was at a low ebb when in 1974, the Defense Advanced Research Agency (DARPA) sent out a request

Above: *Plant 10, the Skunk Works' main facility and headquarters at Palmdale, California.*

Below: **Have Blue 1001 at Burbank prior to being airlifted to Area 51 by USAF C-5A for its first flight on December 1, 1977. (Photos Lockheed)**

Right: *The re-opened U-2R production line at Palmdale in 1982. Note the SR-71s at the back of the hangar.*

to industry for research into a fighter with reduced radar detectability.

The Skunk Works already had experience with designing low observable characteristics into the A-12 and SR-71, and Ben Rich was able to persuade the CIA to release some of the data and the cash-strapped Lockheed board to finance the study.

Rich's team, which included retired Lockheed mathematician Bill Schroeder, came up with an angular concept that reduced the radar cross-section (RCS) significantly more than any other shape.

The investment paid off and in April 1976, Lockheed was selected to build a new aircraft codenamed *Have Blue*.

On December 1, 1977, the first of two prism-shaped technology demonstrators took to the air at Area 51. *Have Blue* 1001 made 36 test flights before being lost when it stalled on landing on May 4 1978. Test pilot Bill Park ejected safely. The second aircraft, 1002, which flew for the first time on July 20, 1978, completed 52 test flights — some of which were flown by USAF pilots — before the programme was successfully completed in 1979. Almost immediately the USAF awarded Lockheed a contract to design and build 20 low observable (LO) subsonic attack aircraft under project *Senior Trend*. The 'stealth' fighter had arrived.

Again, Ben Rich was responsible for the team which designed, built and flew the prototype F-117A in less than three years but the existence of the USAF's first stealth fighter was not officially revealed

for another nine years (see page 42), by which time 51 aircraft had left the Burbank Skunk Works production line.

The F-117A Night Hawk was the last 'black' aircraft to be built at Burbank, all future projects would be designed and assembled at Palmdale. Project *Senior Trend* was

Below: *A Lockheed test pilot wearing the Skunk Works' logo on his flying helmet, straps into an F-117A prior to a test flight from Palmdale. (via Paul Crickmore)*

also the last 'black' Skunk Works programme that has been revealed to date. However, the cutting edge of technology remains the Skunk Works' *raison d'être*. Research and development of the Lockheed Martin F-22 Raptor, and now the X-35 Joint Strike Fighter (JSF) is being carried out at Palmdale which is also heavily involved in space technology and unmanned aerial vehicles.

The Lockheed Martin/Boeing DarkStar UAV is being developed under a contract awarded in 1994. Initial test flights of the first prototype of the stealthy high-altitude vehicle began in 1996 but it was lost on its second flight (see page 72). The second prototype is about to fly.

In 1996, the Skunk Works was selected to lead a multi-industry team to develop the next generation Single-Stage-to-Orbit Reusable Launch vehicle, the X-33 VentureStar, which is being built in the former B-1B plant at Palmdale. It will be powered by linear aerospike rocket motors, an experimental version of which, was built at the Skunk Works and mounted on a NASA SR-71 for flight testing (see page 80). The X-33 subscale demonstrator is scheduled to fly in 1999.

With a growing amount of 'white' programmes, known as *Big Safari* projects, being undertaken the Skunk Works increased its workforce by 1,800 to nearly 6,000 in 1997. Current taskings include re-engineering the U-2Rs, systems integration and modifying C-130 aircraft for electronic warfare, C³, SIGINT (EC-130H Compass Call Block 30) and special operations missions, as well as modifying Argentinean A-4AR Fighting Hawks (See *AFM* News, March 1998).

At the end of the day, the Skunk Works was not so much a building, but a talented and innovative team of engineering and manufacturing people dedicated to the development, production and support of special purpose, high-technology aircraft and systems.

FROM ANGEL
TO
DRAGON LADY

F R O M   A N G E L
D R A G O N   L A D Y

Right: U-2R of OL-UK based at RAF Alconbury in August 1991 soon after the 17th Reconnaissance Wing was deactivated. (Cliff Knox)

Far right: Delivered to the CIA in March 1956, U-2A 56-6682 was later used for carrier operations before being passed to NASA. (Lockheed Martin)

Far right: This rare SAC U-2F with ram's horn antenna, seen at Bien Hoa AB near Saigon in December 1964, was operated by OL-20. (Warren Thompson)

Right: U-2R 68-10337 at RAF Mildenhall in July 1982 assigned to Detachment 4, which was established in April 1979 to operate alongside SR-71s. (AFM-Duncan Cubitt)

Below: Previously classified map of the first CIA-operated U-2 flights over Eastern Europe that took place between June 20 and July 2, 1956. (Lockheed Martin)

Mission 2003   20 June
Mission 2009   2 July
Mission 2010   2 July

The U-2, designed by the Lockheed Skunk Works more than 40 years ago, remains the United States Air Force's primary high-altitude reconnaissance asset which is again taking a frontline role in the latest confrontation with Iraq's Saddam Hussein.

The following is a chronological listing of major events from this remarkable aircraft's long career.

December 9, 1954	Project *Aquatone*, a high-altitude reconnaissance aircraft, is funded by the Central Intelligence Agency (CIA).
July 24, 1955	The first prototype, 'Article 341' is moved from the Skunk Works at Burbank to Area 51 at Groom Lake in a USAF C-124 Globemaster.
August 1, 1955	Article 341, known as 'The Angel', makes its first flight from Area 51 piloted by Lockheed Chief Test Pilot Tony LeVier. He found it difficult to land.
December 1955	CIA pilots converted at Groom Lake on the first of 20 production U-2A aircraft, all of which were built at 'Unit 80' at Oildale, California.
February 1956	U-2A crashed at Groom Lake following failure to release the pogo outriggers on take-off, killing pilot Wilbur Rose.
April 1956	Four U-2s arrive at RAF Lakenheath.
May 1956	The four U-2s and seven CIA pilots move to Weisbaden, West Germany. The unit was called Detachment A.
July 4, 1956	Article 347, a U-2 of Detachment A, piloted by Hervey Stockman, made the first covert flight over Eastern Europe.

Top left: A total of eight RoCAF-operated U-2s were reported to have been shot down over mainland China, four of which are seen here in Beijing. (A J Wnlg)

Above left: CIA pilot Gary Powers, who was shot down over the Soviet Union in a U-2A on July 1, 1960. (Lockheed Martin)

July 5, 1956	Carmen Vito flew the first U-2 flight over Moscow.
September 1956	Two U-2s and seven CIA pilots of Detachment B arrive at Incirlik in Turkey.
September 17, 1956	A U-2A of WRSP-1 (Det A) crashed near Kaiserlautern in West Germany.
February 1957	Two U-2s and seven CIA pilots of Detachment C arrive at Atsugi, Japan.
April 4, 1957	Article 341, the U-2 prototype crashed near Pioche, Nevada killing Lockheed test pilot Bob Sieker.
June 11, 1957	First USAF U-2A assigned to the 4080th SRW at Laughlin AFB, Texas.
June 1957	Lockheed moved the U-2 test operations from Groom Lake to North Base at Edwards AFB, California.
September 24, 1959	Article 360, the first U-2C of WRSP-2 (Det C) belly landed at Fusigawa, Japan.
May 1, 1960	Article 360, U-2C 56-6693, piloted by Gary Powers shot down near Sverdlovsk after being damaged by an SA-2 surface-to-air missile.
June 1960	Detachment D, U-2 headquarters squadron, moved from Groom Lake to North Base at Edwards AFB and the U-2 test operations moved to Burbank.
January 1961	Detachment H established at Taoyuan Air Base near Taipai with two U-2s flown by Republic of China Air Force (RoCAF) pilots.
September 9, 1962	U-2C flown by Col Chen Huai Sheng of the Republic of China Air Force (RoCAF) shot down over eastern China.
October 27, 1962	U-2A 56-6711 of the 4080th SRW shot down over Cuba by an SA-2 SAM killing pilot Maj Rudolf Anderson.
November 20, 1962	U-2C of the 4080th SRW crashed off Key West, Florida.
November 1, 1963	U-2C flown by Maj Yei Chang of the RoCAF shot down near Shanghai.
February 1964	U-2s arrive at Bien Hoa Air Base, South Vietnam — the first USAF types to operate in Southeast Asia.
July 7, 1964	U-2C 3514 flown by Lt Col Terry Lee of the RoCAF shot down over the South China Sea.
August 14, 1964	U-2A 56-6955 flown by RoCAF pilot crashed near Boise, Idaho.
January 10, 1965	U-2C/G 3512 flown by Maj Jack Chang of the RoCAF shot down south of Beijing.

Right: U-2R N812X landed on the carrier USS America in November 1969. (Lockheed Martin)

Right: SAC U-2F 56-66680 operated by the 4080H SRW at OL-20 at Bien Hoa, South Vietnam. (Pete West)

U-2A/D SPECIFICATION

Length	49ft 8in (15.16m)
Span	80ft 2in (24.44m)
Height	15ft 2in (4.63m)
Empty weight	14,250lb (6,464kg)
Max take-off weight	24,150lb (10,954kg)
Maximum speed	430mph (629km/h)
Operational ceiling	70,000+ft (21,650+m)
Maximum range	3,000+ miles (4,828+km)
Powerplant	1x15,800lb st Pratt & Whitney J75-P-13 turbojet

Far left: For comparison, U-2C N804X is parked alongside U-2R N810X (which was later written-off in Cyprus) at Edwards AFB North Base in 1970. (Lockheed Martin)

Left: U-2s that operated from Saudi Arabia during Operation Desert Storm returned wearing seldom-seen tail-art. (AI-Malcolm English)

U-2R (U-2S) SPECIFICATION

Length	62ft 10 1/2in (19.20m)
Span	103ft (31.39m)
Height	16ft (4.88m)
Empty weight	15,000lb (6,805kg)
Max take-off weight	37,150lb (16,851kg)
Maximum speed	430mph (692km/h)
Operational ceiling	78,000ft (23,775m)
Maximum range	6,500miles (12,040km)
Powerplant	1x17,00lb st Pratt & Whitney J75-13B tur bojet (18,300lb st General Electric F101- GE-F29turbofan).

June 1966	U-2 unit, the 4080th SRW, moved to Davis-Monthan AFB, Arizona and was re-numbered the 100th SRW.
July 28, 1966	U-2C of the 100th SRW crashed in Bolivia after overflying Nicaragua.
October 8, 1966	U-2A 56-6690 of the 100th crashed at Bien Hoa, South Vietnam.
1967-8	Twelve new U-2Rs built at Palmdale.
June 9, 1967	U-2C flown by the RoCAF shot down over eastern China.
March 1, 1969	U-2C flown by the RoCAF shot down over Inner Mongolia.
July 1970	USAF U-2Rs arrive at U-Tapao Air Base in Thailand.
November 24, 1970	U-2R 68-10335 flown by Capt Denny Huang of the RoCAF crashed at Taoyuan.
May 29, 1975	U-2C 56-6700 of the 349th SRS crashed near Winterberg, West Germany.
August 15, 1975	U-2R 68-10334 of the 99th SRS crashed in the Gulf of Siam.
December 7, 1977	U-2R 68-10330 of the 99th SRS crashed at RAF Akrotiri, Cyprus.
April 1979	U-2R of Detachment 4 arrived at RAF Mildenhall.
July 15 1981	The first TR-1A, 80-1066 rolled off the re-opened U-2R line at Palmdale.
September 15, 1981	First TR-1A assigned to the 9th SRW/4029th SRS at Beale AFB, California.
February 1983	TR-1As deployed to the 17th Reconnaissance Wing at RAF Alconbury.
May 22, 1984	U-2R 68-10333 of Det 2 crashed at Osan.
July 18, 1984	U-2R of the 9th SRW crashed at Beale AFB.
August 1990	Six TR-1As and six U-2Rs deployed to the 1704th Reconnaissance Squadron (Provisional) at Taif in Saudi Arabia and flew 520 missions during Operations *Desert Shield* and *Desert Storm*.
January 15, 1992	U-2R 68-10332 of the 9th SRW crashed off the coast of North Korea.
December 13, 1993	U-2R 68-10339 of the 9th SRW crashed at Beale AFB.
August 14, 1994	U-2R 80-1098 crashed at Det 2's Osan base.
March 15,1995	U-2Rs of OL-UK moved from Alconbury to RAF Fairford.
August 28, 1995	U-2R 68-10338 crashed at RAF Fairford due to non release of outrigger pogo.
January 1, 1996	U-2Rs deployed to Istres in France with OL-FR to join IFOR monitoring over Bosnia.
August 7, 1996	U-2R 80-1088 of the 9th SRW crashed near Beale AFB.
November 1997	U-2Rs of the 4402nd (Provisional) Squadron move from Taif to Al Kharj, Saudi Arabia.

100% MODERN MILITARY AVIATION

AirForces Monthly is devoted to 100% modern military aircraft. It has built up a formidable reputation by getting to places where other military aviation magazines only think about. *AirForces Monthly* has been there, taken photographs and captured world exclusive features long before others hear whispers. *AirForces Monthly's* reputation is unrivalled worldwide.

Unbiased on it's reporting on the world's air forces and their airpower, *AirForces Monthly* leads the way on potential "hotspots areas" and the airpower available to resolve certain situations. *AirForces Monthly* is constantly updating the strengths of airforces, their conflicts, weaponry, exercises, retirements, and cut-backs throughout the world. There's the latest write-offs, collisions, losses and worldwide accidents reports. Overall, an unrivalled combination of up-to-the-minute news coverage, superb photography, and in-depth reporting from all over the globe makes *AirForces Monthly* one of the world's leading aviation magazines.

AirForces Monthly is on sale the second Thursday of every month. To guarantee that you don't miss out on a single issue ask your newsagent to reserve you a copy.

For information on the latest subscription offers direct from the publishers, or for back issues enquiries contact: *AirForces Monthly*, Key Direct Ltd., PO Box 300, Stamford, Lincs., PE9 1NA. United Kingdom. Telephone: 01780 480404 Fax: 01780 757261 E-Mail: orders@keymags.demon.co.uk

http://www.keymags.co.uk

KEY PUBLISHING

Operation OXCART

Left: The second Lockheed YF-12A-LO, 60-6936, flying over Death Valley piloted by Jim Eastham (Lockheed Martin)

FROM EARLY JULY 1956 the U-2 and its reconnaissance gathering systems, became the pre-eminent means of gathering strategically vital intelligence concerning the USSR and its satellites. However, despite spectacular results, the Killian Committee — a Department of Defense (DoD) sponsored think-tank, was concerned about the Soviets' ability to accurately track on radar the subsonic U-2, correctly predicting that it was only a question of time before a successful intercept occurred.

Accordingly, Richard Bissell, the Central Intelligence Agency's (CIA) Special Assistant for Planning and Co-ordination began organising research and development of follow-on systems. In the autumn of 1957, he contacted 'Kelly' Johnson and asked if the Lockheed Skunk Works team would conduct an operations analysis into the relationship of interceptability and an aircraft's speed, altitude and its radar cross section (RCS). As Kelly was already immersed in related studies, he agreed to accept the project, the results of which concluded that supersonic speed coupled with the use of radar attenuating materials (RAM) and radar attenuating design greatly reduced, but not negated, chances of

Paul Crickmore looks at the development of the world's first Mach 3 combat aircraft.

radar detection. During the closing months of 1957, the Agency invited Lockheed Aircraft Corporation and the Convair Division of General Dynamics to field design submissions to them for a reconnaissance gathering vehicle which adhered to the afore-

Left: The CIA A-12 Cygnus patch. (Author)

Above: *One of two A-12s used as a 'mother' aircraft for the D-21 reconnaissance drone, 60-6940 was redesignated M-21. (Lockheed Martin)*

mentioned performance criteria.

Recognising the need for government funding, Bissell recruited and cleared into the programme a team of six specialists under the chair of Dr Edwin Land. Between 1957 and 1959 the panel met on some six occasions, to evaluate the various proposals. Codenamed Project *Gusto* by the Agency, Lockheed's first submission, *Archangel*, proposed a Mach 3 cruise aircraft with a range of 4,000nm (7,400km) at 90-95,000ft (27-29,000m). This, together with his *Gusto* Model G-2A submission, were both well received by the Programme Office.

Convair on the other hand prepared the Super Hustler, which was Mach 4 capable, ramjet powered when launched from a B-58 and turbojet assisted for landing. As designs were refined and re-submitted the Lockheed offerings became shortened to A, followed by an index number, these ran from A-3 to A-12. The design and designations from Convair also evolved and on August 20, 1959, final submissions from both companies were made to a joint DoD/Air Force/CIA selection panel. Though strikingly different in appearance, the proposed performance of both aircraft compared

favourably.

On August 28, Kelly was informed that the Skunk Works had won the competition, Project *Gusto* was now at an end and a new codename, *Oxcart*, was assigned. The technical challenge facing the Skunk Works team was vast, Kelly would later remark that virtually everything on the aircraft had to be invented from scratch. Sustained operation in an extreme temperature environment meant lavish use of advanced titanium alloys which accounted for 85% of the aircraft's structural weight. Chosen powerplant would be the Pratt & Whitney JT11D-

Right: *Ten of the 12 Lockheed A-12s ever built are seen here at Groom Lake in 1963 with the prototype 60-6924 in the foreground next to the two-seat Goose 60-6927. (CIA via Author)*

20 engine (designated J58 by the US military). This high bypass ratio afterburning engine was the result of two earlier, ill-fated programmes; nevertheless, the engine had already completed 700 hours of full-scale engine testing and results were encouraging.

On January 30, 1960, the Agency gave Lockheed ADP the go-ahead to manufacture and test a dozen A-12s, including one two-seat conversion trainer. Construction work at the jets' secret test site in Nevada, Area 51, Groom Lake, referred to variously as 'the Ranch' or 'the Area' also got under way. A new 8,500ft (2,600m) runway was constructed, and three US Navy hangars together with Navy housing units were transported to the site in readiness for the arrival of the A-12 prototype, expected in May 1961. However, problems experienced by Pratt & Whitney soon began to compound and the anticipated first flight date slipped to late February 1962, although even then the J58 would still not be ready. Eventually Kelly decided that J75 engines would be used in the interim to propel the A-12 to a 'half-way house' of 50,000ft (15,240m) and Mach 1.6. The flightcrew selection process got under way in 1961 and on completion the first pilots were: William Skliar, Kenneth Collins, Walter Ray, Alonzo Walter, Mele

Vojvodich, Jack Weeks, Jack Layton, Dennis Sullivan, David Young, Francis Murray and Russ Scott. In the spring of 1962 eight F-101 Voodoos, to be used as companion trainers and chase aircraft, arrived at the remote base. A large 'restricted airspace zone' was enforced by the Federal Aviation Authority (FAA), and security measures were invoked upon radar controllers to ensure that fast-moving targets seen on their screens were not discussed. Planned air refuelling operations of *Oxcart* aircraft would be conducted by the 903rd Air Refuelling Squadron located at Beale AFB, equipped with KC-135Q tankers which possessed separate 'clean' tankage and plumbing to isolate the A-12's JP7 fuel from the tanker's JP4. These tankers also carried special ARC-50 distance-ranging radios for use in precision, long distance, high-speed join ups with the A-12s.

The first A-12 was crated, covered with canvas and left Burbank by trailer at 2.30am on February 26, 1962; it arrived safely at Area 51, two days later. On April 24, Lou Schalk took the aircraft on a high-speed taxi run that culminated in a momentary lift off and landing roll-out onto the dry, salty lake-bed. Two days later he completed the *Oxcart's* first full flight — a faultless 0705am take-off was followed shortly thereafter by all the left wing fillets

Left: *CIA A-12 Oxcart pilot Kenneth Collins whose callsign was 'Dutch 21'.* (Author)

being shed. Constructed from RAM, luckily these elements were non-structural and Lou recovered the aircraft back at Groom Dry Lake without further incident. Flight testing was dogged by problems and delays. On April 30 — nearly a year behind schedule, Lou took the A-12 on its 'official' first flight. The 59 minute flight took the aircraft to a top speed and altitude of 340kts (630km/h) and 30,000ft (9,140m). Four days later the aircraft went supersonic for the first time, reaching Mach 1.1. Lockheed test pilot Bill Park joined the team shortly thereafter, and on June 26 the second A-12 arrived at Area 51 and was immediately assigned to a three-month static test programme. The third and fourth aircraft arrived during October and November, the latter was a two-seat A-12 trainer — nicknamed the *Goose* by its crews — and it was powered throughout its life by two J58s. On October 5 another milestone was achieved when the A-12 flew for the first time with a J58, (a J75 was retained in the right nacelle until January 15, 1963, when the first fully J58 powered flight took place).

On October 27, 1962, Maj Rudolph Anderson was killed when his aircraft was shot down by an SA-2 while monitoring Soviet ballistic missile build-ups during the Cuban missile crisis. Just like the Gary Powers shoot-down two and a half years earlier, the U-2's vulnerability had been demonstrated in a spectacular fashion. The significance of the incident was certainly not lost on intelligence communities involved in *Oxcart* and the successful prosecution of that programme now became a matter of highest national priority.

AF-12

During December 1960, a separate project group was organised in the Skunk Works, running independently of the A-12 team. The entire forward

fuselage forebody of an A-12 would be modified to create a Mach 3.2 interceptor. Originally designated AF-12, the aircraft was equipped with the Hughes AN/ASG-18 pulse Doppler radar and the GAR-9 (later redesignated AIM 47) missile system, originally intended for the cancelled North American F-108 Rapier. On May 31 the Air Force conducted a mock-up review of the AF-12 and was duly impressed. By June, wind tunnel tests revealed directional stability problems resulting from the revised nose configuration. As a result, a large folding fin was mounted under the aft fuselage as were two shorter fixed fins beneath each nacelle. A bomber version of the A-12, designated the RB-12, also reached the mock-up stage, but this would prove to be still-born, as it represented too much of a threat to the highly political North American XB-70A Valkyrie. On August 7, 1963, several weeks after being moved to Groom Lake, Jim Eastham climbed aboard the interceptor prototype and took 60-6934 (the seventh A-12) for its first flight, a flight he would later modestly describe as a 'typical production test flight'.

In November 1963, President Johnson was briefed on the programme, after which Kelly Johnson noted, "Plans going forward for surfacing of the AF-12 programme. I worked on the draft to be used by President Johnson and proposed the terminology 'A-11' as it was the non-anti-radar version."

On Saturday February 29, 1964, prior to the President announcing the existence of part of the programme, two AF-12s, 60-6934 and 60-6935, were flown from Groom Lake to Edwards AFB, by Lou Schalk and Bill Park, thereby diverting attention away from Area 51 and the 'black world' A-12 programme. Now an Air Force programme, the interceptor's designation was changed to YF-12A.

The third YF-12A, 60-6936, soon joined the other two at Edwards as Jim Eastham continued the envelope extension programme. On March 18, 1965, YF-12A '935 successfully engaged a Q-2C target drone at 40,000ft (12,000m), while the interceptor flew at Mach 2.2 and 65,000ft (19,800m).

Aware of the number of world speed and altitude records held by the USSR, the DoD informed Kelly of its desire to use the YF-12A to wrestle several of those records off the Soviets. Accordingly, on May 1, 1965 (five years to the day that Gary Powers was shot down in his U-2 by a Soviet SA-2), six records were smashed by 60-6936.

Following a Senate Armed Services Committee hearing into the future of continental air defence, it was decided, in the light of intelligence available at the time, to downgrade Aerospace Defense Command, which in turn rendered the F-12B (proposed production variant of the YF-12A), unnecessary. Consequently, on January 5, 1968, official notification was received from the Air Force to 'close down the F-12B'; the YF-12A programme was formally ended on February 1.

And so it fell to the 'black world' A-12 *Oxcart* programme to validate the concept of high-altitude, sustained Mach 3-plus flight in an operational environment. By late 1965, all of the Agency pilots were Mach 3 qualified and the A-12 was ready for operational testing. Despite this, political sensitivities surrounding the Gary Powers' shoot down five years earlier conspired to ensure that the aircraft would never carry out missions over the USSR — the very country it was originally built to overfly. The initial answer as to where to deploy this multi-million dollar national security asset was Cuba.

On August 5, 1965, the director of the National Security Agency, directed

that Operation *Skylark* achieve emergency operational readiness by November 5, this capability was achieved, but never deployed; instead *Cygnus*, as Agency pilots referred to the A-12, would receive its baptism of fire in the skies over South East Asia. Over the next 18 months, several requests to deploy *Cygnus* to the Far East were made, but it was not until May 1967 that matters came to a head. The National Security Council was briefed that North Vietnam was about to receive surface-to-surface ballistic missiles. Richard Helms of the CIA proposed that the 303 Committee authorise deployment of *Oxcart*, as it was ideally equipped to carry out the task, having a superior camera to that used by U-2s or pilotless drones and being 'invulnerable to shoot-downs'. President Johnson approved the plan and in mid-May an airlift was begun to establish Operation *Black Shield* at Kadena AB on Okinawa.

To War

At 0800 on May 22, 1967, Mel Vojvodich deployed A-12 60-6937 from Area 51 to Okinawa during a flight which lasted six hours, six minutes and included three air refuellings. Two days later, Jack Layton joined Mele in 60-6930; and 60-6932 flown by Jack Weeks arrived on Okinawa on the 27th, having been forced to divert

Left: A-12 60-6928, seen here at Edwards AFB, is wearing the type's definitive matt black overall colour scheme. (Author)

into Wake Island for a day following INS and radio problems.

On May 31 despite torrential rain, conditions over 'the collection area' were good and at 0800 Kadena received a final 'go' from Washington. On cue, Mel engaged both afterburners and made an instrument-guided take-off. A few minutes later he burst through cloud and flew 60-6937 up to 25,000ft (7,600m) and topped-off the tanks from a KC-135. Disengaged from the '135's boom he accelerated and climbed to operational speed and altitude having informed Kadena ('homeplate') that aircraft systems were running as per the book and the back-up services of Jack Layton would not be required. Mel penetrated hostile airspace at Mach 3.2 and 80,000ft (24,380m); the so-called 'front door' entry was made over Haiphong, then Hanoi, exiting North Vietnam near Dien Bien Phu. A second air refuelling took place over Thailand, followed by another climb to altitude and a second penetration of North Vietnamese airspace made near the Demilitarised Zone (DMZ), after which he recovered the aircraft following three instrument approaches in driving rain, back at Kadena.

In all the flight had lasted three hours and 40 minutes, several SA-2s were fired at the aircraft but all detonated above and well behind their target. The 'photo-take' was downloaded and sent by a special courier aircraft to the Eastman Kodak plant in Rochester, New York, for processing. In all '937's large camera, located in the Q-bay behind the pilot, successfully photographed ten priority target categories including 70 of the 190 known SAM sites. By mid-July A-12 overflights had determined, with a high degree of confidence, that there were no surface-to-surface missiles in North Vietnam. During 1967, a total of 41 A-12 missions were alerted, of which 22 were actually granted approval for flight.

Between January 1 and March 31, 1968, 15 missions were alerted, of which six were flown — four over North Vietnam and two over North Korea. The latter two came about following seizure on the night of January 23, of the USS Pueblo — a US Navy Signals Intelligence (SIGINT) vessel — by North Korea. The first sortie was attempted by Jack Weeks on January 25, but a malfunction on the A-12 resulted in an abort shortly after take-off. The next day Frank Murray completed the task, "I left Kadena, topped-off, then entered northern airspace over the Sea of Japan via the Korean Straits. My first pass started off near Vladivostok, then with the camera on I flew down the east coast of North Korea where we thought the boat was. As I approached Wonsan I could see the Pueblo through my view sight. The harbour was all iced up except at the very entrance and there she was, sitting off to the right of the main entrance. I continued to the border with South Korea, completed a 180 degree turn and flew back over North Korea. I made four passes photographing the whole of North Korea from the DMZ to the Yalu border. As far as I know, I was undetected throughout the flight, but when I got back to Kadena some folks told me that the Chinese had detected me and told the North Koreans, but they never reacted." Back at Kadena 'the take' was immediately flown to Yakota AB, Japan, where the 67th Reconnaissance Technical Squadron had been activated to enable the more timely exploitation of such data by theatre commanders.

On May 8, 1968, Jack Laden successfully completed a mission over North Korea; it was to prove the final operational flight of an A-12. A long-standing debate concerning whether the A-12 or a programme known as Senior Crown, should carry forward the strategic reconnaissance baton, had, after three years been resolved, Oxcart was vanquished. In early March 1968, SR-71s began arriving at Kadena to take over the Black Shield commitment. Those A-12s back at 'the Area' were flown to Palmdale and placed in storage by June 7. At Kadena the three aircraft that had performed all the Black Shield missions were also readied for a return transpacific ferry flight.

On June 2, 1968, tragedy once again hit the Oxcart programme, when Jack Weeks was killed during an Functional Check Flight (FCF) in 60-6932. The aircraft and its pilot were lost without trace in the Pacific Ocean.

The two remaining A-12s on Okinawa, 60-6930 and 60-6937 were ferried back to Area 51, before being flown to Palmdale, the last flight being made by Frank Murray on June 21, 1968 in aircraft '937.

Left: YF-12 '934 wearing the USAF's Systems Command badge on the fin, is seen with its ventral fin extended and missile-launch camera pods under the engine nacelles. (Lockhed Martin)

Right: *The supersonic D-21 drone riding 'piggy-back' on A-12 60-6940 that was redesignated M-21.*

Paul Crickmore looks at the follow-on 'Black' project from the Kelly Johnson stable — the super-sonic unmanned recce drone, the D-21.

MOTHER & DAUGHTER
- Project Tagboard

ON OCTOBER 10, 1962, Kelly Johnson received authorisation from the CIA to carry out study work on a drone that would be mated with an A-12. At the root of such a request was the US Government's decision to discontinue overflight activity, following the Gary Powers shoot-down.

Progress was rapid, on December 7 a full-scale mock-up was completed of the craft, which within the Skunk Works was referred to as the Q-12.

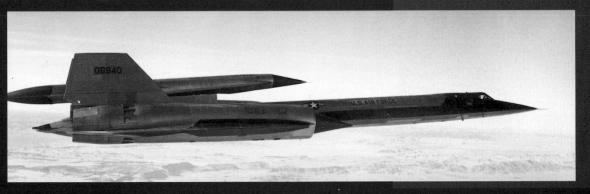

Right: *The Mach 3 D-21A recce drone, here fitted with frangible nose and tail cones, proved difficult to launch from the M-21, one being lost during trials.*

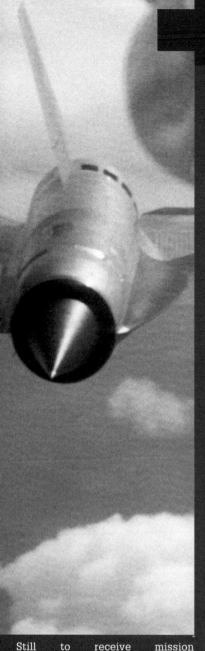

21 flew its sortie independently. Equipped with an inertial navigation system (INS), the D-21 would fly a pre-programmed flight profile, execute turns, camera on/off points to produce the perfect photo-recce sortie. Having completed its camera run, the drone's INS system then sent signals to the auto-pilot system to descend to a predetermined 'feet wet' film collection point. The entire palletised unit containing INS, camera and film, was then ejected at 60,000ft (18,280m) and Mach 1.67 and parachuted towards the ocean. As the drone continued its descent, it was blown apart by a barometrically activated explosive charge. Meanwhile, air retrieval was executed by a JC-130B Hercules. On August 12, 1964, the first M-21 was dispatched to Groom Dry Lake and on December 22 the first D-21/M-21 combination flight took place with Bill Park at the controls. Troubles, however, dogged *Tagboard* and the fourth and final D-21 sortie from the M-21 occurred on July 30, 1966. It ended in disaster when the drone collided with '941 moments after achieving launch separation. The impact caused the mother craft to pitch up so violently that the fuselage forebody broke off. Both Bill Park and his LCO, Ray Torick, successfully ejected and made a 'feet wet' landing, but unfortunately Torick's pressure suit filled with water and he drowned before he could be rescued. Bill Park spent an hour in the ocean before he was

brought aboard a US Navy vessel.

The D-21 was grounded for a year whilst a new launch system was developed. This new operation, code-named *Senior Bowl,* involved the drone being launched from the underwing pylons of two modified B-52Hs of the 4200th Test Wing based at Beale AFB. Upon launch, the D-21B was accelerated to Mach 3.3 and 80,000ft (24,380m) by a solid propellant rocket and on achieving cruise speed and altitude the booster was jettisoned and the drone's flight continued, as described earlier. The first launch attempt from a BUFF was made on November 6, 1967, but proved unsuccessful, as did three other attempts. Success was finally achieved on June 16, 1968. Between November 9, 1969, and March 20, 1971, a total of four operational flights over China were attempted, achieving only limited success *Senior Bowl* was cancelled on July 15, 1971.

Above: *The operational D-21B with its solid fuel rocket booster was carried by modified B-52Hs of the 4200th Test Wing based at Beale AFB. (Lockheed Martin)*

Still to receive mission specifications from the Agency, Kelly worked on producing a vehicle with a range of 3,000nm (5,560km) hauling a Hycon camera system, capable of a photographic resolution of 6in from operating altitude. The engine to be used was the Marquardt RJ43 — MA-3 Bomarc, and by October 1963 the overall configuration for the Q-12 and its launch platform — two purpose-built, modified A-12s, were nearing completion. Codenamed *Tagboard,* the designation of both elements was also changed, the carrier vehicle became the 'M' - standing for 'Mother' 21 and the Q-12 became the 'D' - for 'Daughter' 21.

The 11,000lb (5,000kg) D-21 was supported on the M-21 by a single, dorsally-mounted pylon. Reaching launch point, the mothership's pilot maintained Mach 3.12 and initiated a -0.9 of a 'g' push over, once released by the Launch Control Officer (LCO) sitting in what was on other A-12 aircraft, the Q bay, the D-

Left: *D-21B launch sequence.*

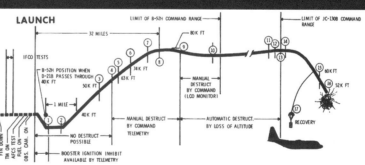

D-21B Sequence of Events

BOOSTER IGNITION-	5 DESTRUCT ALTITUDE SWITCH OPEN	9 AUTOMATIC DESTRUCT CIRCUITRY ARM	14 FUEL "OFF"
5° PITCH-UP, FOLLOWED BY 1°/SEC PULL-UP	6 ENGINE IGNITION: AUTO DESTRUCT CIRCUIT COMPLETE	10 COMMAND AND T/M "OFF"	15 EJECT HATCH
TRANSITION TO FINAL CLIMB TRAJECTORY	7 APU LOAD TAKE-OVER	11 COMMAND "ON"	16 AUTOMATIC DESTRUCT
MANUAL DESTRUCT CIRCUIT COMPLETE	8 BOOSTER JETTISON, AFCS TO MACH HOLD	12 BEACONS "ON" AND T/M "ON"	17 HATCH RECOVERY
		13 DESTRUCT DISABLE	

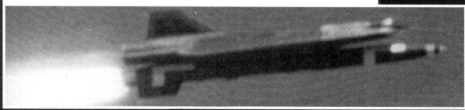

OPERATION SENIOR CROWN

Left: *SR-71 Blackbird 64-17971 of the 9th RW Det 1 at Edwards AFB flying one of its last operational USAF sorties in July 1997 before the type was finally withdrawn from service. (Ted Carlson)*

The world's fastest operational aircraft, the SR-71 Blackbird, operated over the world's 'hot spots' for more than 30 years. Paul Crickmore reports.

WHILE WORKING ON *Oxcart* back in the early spring of 1962, Kelly Johnson had mentioned the possibility of producing a reconnaissance/strike variant for the Air Force. By the end of April, two different mock-ups were under construction referred to as the R-12 and RS-12. On February 18, 1963, Lockheed received precontractual authority to build six R-12 aircraft (later designated SR-71 by the Air Force), with the understanding that 25 aircraft would be ordered by July 1. The RS-12 and later the B-12/B71 proposals for a strike version of the aircraft would fail to win production contracts, despite Kelly having demonstrated to the Air Force the unique capabilities of such a platform. In a speech made on July 24, 1964, President Johnson revealed to the world the existence of the SR-71.

The prototype SR-71A, serial 64-17950 (article number 2001), was delivered by truck from Burbank to Site 2, Air Force Plant 42, Building 210, at Palmdale, for final assembly, on October 29, 1964. With two J58s installed, Chief Test Pilot, Bob Gilliland conducted '950's first engine test run on December 18, 1964. Three days later, a 'no-flight' was conducted where Gilliland accelerated the aircraft to 120kts (222km/h) before snapping the throttles back to idle and deploying the large 40ft (12m) drag chute. Four days later, Gilliland (using his personal callsign *Dutch 51*), got airborne from runway 25 at Palmdale in SR-71A, 64-17950. The back seat or Reconnaissance Systems Officer's (RSO) position remained empty on this historic flight for safety reasons, during the course of which Bob reached an altitude of 50,000ft (15,240m) and a speed of Mach 1.5.

Aircraft '951 and '952 were added to the test fleet for

Right: The first flight of SR-71 64-17950 at Palmdale on December 22, 1964 with Bob Gilliland at the controls, followed by an F-104A chase plane. (Lockheed Martin)

contractor development of payload systems and techniques, and shortly after the Phase II Developmental Test Programme was started, four other Lockheed test pilots were brought into the project: Jim Eastham, Bill Weaver, Art Peterson and Darrell Greenamyer.

Developmental efforts within Lockheed were matched by Air Force Systems Command (AFSC) which structured a 'Development and Evaluation Programme' that would evaluate the new aircraft for the Air Force. This programme was undertaken by the SRO-71/YF 12 Test Force at the Air Force Flight Test Center, Edwards AFB. Both Phase 1 'Experimental' and Phase II 'Development' test flying had moved to Edwards where SR-71As '953, '954 and '955 were to be evaluated by the 'blue suiters'.

Beale AFB in California, chosen for

the newcomer, underwent an $8.4 million construction programme and on January 1, 1965, the 4200th Strategic Reconnaissance Wing (SRW) was activated. The first two of eight Northrop T-38 Talons arrived at Beale on July 7, 1965, these would be used as 'companion trainers' to maintain overall flying proficiency for the SR-71 crew. On January 7, 1966 the first of two SR-71Bs were delivered to Beale AFB, this was followed five months later by their first 'A' model, 64-17958. On June 25, 1966, the 4200th was redesignated the 9th SRW, its component flying squadrons being the 1st and 99th Strategic Reconnaissance Squadrons (SRS). Crew training and Category III Operational Testing proceeded in earnest but was not without cost.

With the Agency operating its small fleet of Oxcart aircraft, it was inevitable that the question 'Do we need both systems?' was asked. On December 12, 1966, following the results of a trip-agency study and subsequent vote, a decision was reached to 'terminate the Oxcart fleet in January 1968 and assign all missions to the SR-71 fleet'. This was transmitted to President Johnson, who accepted the Bureau of the Budget recommendations and directed that the Oxcart programme

be terminated by January 1, 1968. In the event, the Oxcart run-down lagged, but the original decision to terminate the programme was reaffirmed on May 16, 1968.

OL-8

As the 1 SRS neared operational readiness, it was decided that three aircraft and four crews would be deployed to Okinawa, the fourth crew would be stand-by for the three deploying aircraft and would arrive at Kadena — if their services were not needed — by KC-135Q tanker. Two days before Glowing Heat, the codename for the deployment, six KC-135Q tankers were positioned at Hickam AFB, Hawaii. Emergency radio coverage was set up on Wake Island and on March 8, 1968, Maj Buddy Brown and his RSO Dave Jenson left Beale in '978 and became the first Senior Crown crew deployed to the war zone. Two days later Maj Jerry O'Malley and Capt Ed Payne delivered '976 to the OF. They were followed on March 13 by Bob Spencer and Keith Branham in '974. Finally, three days later in late evening rain, Jim Watkins and Dave Dempster, the back-up crew, arrived in the '135 — the crews and their mounts were ready for business. During Kadena-based operations the SR-71 received

Above: Maj Jerry O'Malley (pilot) and Capt Ed Payne (RSO) flew the first operational mission from Kadena in SR-71 '967 on March 21, 1968. (via Author)

Right: An early photograph of an SR-71 in the shed at Edwards AFB with its sideways-looking airborne radar (SLAR) revealed during maintenance. (Lockheed Martin)

its nickname, *Habu*, after a poisonous pit viper found on the Ryuku Islands — it is a name which has proved to be permanent amongst all associated with *Senior Crown*.

The first crew to fly the SR-71 operationally was Maj Jerry O'Malley and Capt Ed Payne in '976. The mission was flown Thursday March 21, 1968 and their route was similar to that flown by Mel Vojvodich in his A-12, ten months earlier. However, for its first operational mission, the SR-71 carried a downward-looking Terrain Objective Camera, in the chine bays were the left and right long focal-length 'close-look' Technical Objective 'TEOC', or 'Tech' cameras. Behind these, were two Operational Objective Cameras (OOCs), but of greater significance was the Goodyear Side-Looking Airborne Radar (SLAR) located in the detachable nose section, and its associated AR-1700 radar recorder unit found within the right chine.

All went well until arrival back at Kadena where Jerry and Ed were confronted with a base completely 'fogged in'. Despite a good Ground Controlled Approach (GCA), Jerry never saw the runway and had to divert to Taiwan. In company with two tankers the three-ship formation made its slow, lumbering way to Ching Chuan Kang. On arrival, the SR-71 was quickly hangared and the next day the 'take' down loaded and despatched for processing — the film to the 67th

RTS at Yokota AB, Japan and the SLAR imagery to the 9th RTS at Beale AFB. After two nights in Taiwan Jerry and Ed ferried '976 back to Kadena. Post mission intelligence results were stunning. The SLAR imagery had revealed the location of many artillery emplacements around Khe Sanh, and a huge truck park which was used to support the guns, these sites had eluded US sensors on other recce aircraft, and over the next few days air strikes were mounted against both targets, reducing their effectiveness dramatically. After a 77-day siege, Khe Sanh was at last relieved on April 7, 1968 (two weeks after '976's discovery sortie). As a result of their highly successful mission, both Maj

O'Malley and Capt Payne were awarded the Distinguished Flying Cross. On its very first operational mission the SR-71 had proved its value.

Of the 168 SR-71 sorties flown by OL-8 throughout 1968, 67 were operational missions over North Vietnam, the remaining sorties being FCFs or for crew training. In addition, the first of many aircraft change overs took place.

On the night of September 27, 1971, Majs Bob Spencer and Butch Sheffield completed post take-off tanking and established '980 on a northerly track. US Intelligence had obtained details of the largest ever Soviet naval exercise to be held near Vladivostok, in the Sea of Japan; such an event could prove a rich

Above & left: SR-71 64-17974 of the 9th SRW named Ichi Ban, was one of four Blackbirds to undertake the first operational deployment to OL-8 at Kadena in 1968. (Photo -Whitaker/ Thompson. Art-work - Pete West)

Below: Seen lifting off from a damp and humid Kadena Air Base, Japan, in 1970 is 9th SRW Black-bird 64-17975. (Whitaker/ Thompson)

BENINA AIRFIELD
15 APR 86

DESTROYED F-27

DAMAGED MI-8/HIP

DESTROYED MI-8/HIP

Right: An image of Benina Airfield in Libya taken by an SR-71 of Det 4 from RAF Mildenhall following the US bombing raids in April 1986.

Right: Operation Eldorado Canyon mission markings on SR-71 64-17980, the first Blackbird over Libya following the bombing of military airfields in Tripoli and Benghazi. (Photos via Author)

fishing ground for an intelligence data trawl and the *Habu* was an ideal vehicle for stirring up the Soviet fleet's defence systems. In addition, national security officials were especially interested in obtaining signal details relating to the Soviet's new SA-5 SAM system, and as '980 bore down on the target area, dozens of Soviet radars were switched on. Just short of entering Soviet airspace the *Habu* rolled into a 35° banked turn, remaining throughout in international airspace. However, on approach to the target area, he noted the right engine's oil pressure was dipping. Clearing the area, Bob discovered the reading had fallen to 'zero'. He shut down the engine and was forced to descend and decelerate to subsonic speeds. They were now sitting ducks for any Soviet fast jets sent up to intercept the oil-starved *Habu*. Worse still, at lower altitude they were subjected to strong headwinds which rapidly depleted their fuel supply. Recovery back to Kadena was impossible — instead they would have to divert into South Korea.

The OL commander had been monitoring '980's slow progress and as the *Habu* neared Korea, US listening posts reported the launch of several MiGs from Pyongyang, North Korea. In response USAF F-102s were scrambled from a base near Hon Chew, South Korea and vectored into a position between the *Habu* and the MiGs. It was later established that the MiG launch was unconnected with the *Habu's* descent and Bob recovered '980 into Taegu, South Korea, without further incident. In all, their EMR 'take' had recorded emissions from 290 different radars, but the greatest prize was 'capture' of the much sought after SA-5 signals — a first.

Operations from the USA

At 1400hrs on October 6, 1973, an Egyptian and Syrian artillery barrage spelled the beginning of the Yom Kippur War. In view of the grave situation faced by the Israelis the US decided to step up intelligence efforts and use the SR-71 to provide a hot-spot reconnaissance capability. It was planned that such missions would be flown from Beale across the war zone and recover into RAF Mildenhall, England. However, to safeguard the supply of Arab oil, the Heath government denied the SR-71 use of Mildenhall. Instead round-robin missions would be flown from Griffiss AFB, New York. Accordingly, two SR-71s, '979 and '964, were pre-positioned to that eastern seaboard base. At 0200hrs, October 13, Lt Col Jim Shelton and RSO Maj Gary Coleman departed Griffiss heading east to make good the first of many ARCPs (Air Refuelling Contact Points).

Below: Blackbird 64-17964, belonging to the 9th SRW Det 4, is seen in its hangar at RAF Mildenhall prior to a mission in December 1987. (Author)

Far left: *Seen over RAF Mildenhall in 1986, a Det 4 Blackbird 'lights-up' as excess fuel is burned off. (AFM - Duncan Cubitt)*

Left: *SR-71 64-17974 crashed in the sea on April 21, 1987, while on a mission from Kadena following an engine explosion. The crew, Maj Dan E House and Capt Blair L Bozek, ejected safely. (via Author)*

Topping-off he continued east to the next cell of tankers just beyond the Azores. Returning again to speed and altitude, a high-Mach dash took them through the Straits of Gibraltar and let-down for a third air refuelling just east of the heel of Italy. Due to the proximity of the war zone and Libya, the US Navy provided a CAP (Combat Air Patrol), from carrier-based aircraft on station in the Mediterranean.

They then resumed their climb and acceleration to coast in over Port Said. In all, '979 spent 25 minutes over 'denied territory', entering Egyptian airspace at 1103 GMT, its crew covered the Israeli battle fronts with both Egypt and Syria before coasting out and letting down towards their fourth ARCP, which was still being capped by the US Navy. Their next hot leg was punctuated by a fifth refuelling, again near the Azores, before a final high-speed run across the western

Atlantic towards New York. Mindful of his own fatigue, Gary was in awe of his pilot who completed a text book sixth air refuelling before greasing '979 back down at Griffiss after a combat sortie lasting ten hours 18 minutes (more than five hours of which was at Mach 3 or above) and involving 11 tanking operations from the ever dependable KC-135Qs.

Their reconnaissance 'take' was of 'high quality' and provided intelligence and defence analysts with much-needed information concerning the diposition of Arab

Left: *With landing gear down and landing light on, a Det 4 SR-71 crosses the Mildenhall threshold prior to touch-down.*

forces in the region which was then made available to the Israelis. In all, eight further SR-71 sorties were flown over the region. The sorties stand as a testament of the long reach capability to the aircraft and its ability to operate, at short notice, with impunity in a high threat environment.

Det 4 Mildenhall

As noted earlier the first planned visit of an SR-71 to England was to have been October 11, 1973, during the Yom Kippur War, instead it was not until September 9, 1974 when

Left: *A Det 4 Blackbird powers off the Mildenhall runway with full afterburners. (Photos AFM-Duncan Cubitt)*

Majs Jim Sullivan and Noel Widdifield, flying '972 established a new New York to London transatlantic speed record of less than two hours. Eighteen months later, '972 returned as *Burns 31* and flew two aborted missions in a bid to obtain SLAR imagery of the Soviet Northern fleet. After nearly two years of these short TDY deployments, Detachment 4 (Det 4) of the 9th SRW was activated at RAF Mildenhall to support U-2R and SR-71 operations on March 31, 1979. It was these Peace-time Aerial Reconnaissance Operations (PAROP) to monitor the Soviet Northern fleet that provided the SR-71 programme with an important *modus operandi,* at a time when the budgetary axe was being wielded. There were, however, several notable exceptions to this fertile hunting ground, one being the Middle East. Tension between the United States and much of the Arab world continued, and after a series of incidents, President Reagan's patience snapped.

On April 15, 1986, Operation *Eldorado Canyon,* a coordinated strike on targets in Libya by air elements of the US Navy and 18 USAF F-111s from RAF Lakenheath, was mounted. Lt Cols Jerry Glasser and Ron Tabor took off from Mildenhall as scheduled at 0500hrs in SR-71 '980 (callsign *Tromp 30*). Their mission was to secure photographic imagery for post-strike bomb damage assessment. To achieve this it would be necessary to overfly those targets hit earlier, but this time in broad daylight and with the

sophisticated Libyan defence network on full alert. Such was the importance of the mission that SR-71A '960 (*Tromp 31*) flown by Majs Brian Shul and Walt Watson, launched at 0615 hrs as an airborne spare should *Tromp 30* abort with platform or sensor problems. In the event all aircraft systems, the two chine-mounted Technical Objective Cameras (TEOCs) for spot coverage and the nose-mounted Optical Bar Cameras (OBC) for horizon-to-horizon coverage worked as advertised aboard the primary aircraft and '960 was not called upon to penetrate hostile airspace. Despite launches against '980, the SR-71 again proved that it could operate with impunity against such SAM threats and at 0935hrs *Tromp 30* landed safely back at 'the

Hall'. The mission's 'take' was processed in the MPC located within one of Mildenhall's disused hangars. It was then transported by a KC-135 (*Trout 99*) to Andrews AFB, Maryland, where national-level officials were eagerly awaiting post-strike briefings.

Two further missions over Libya were conducted on April 16 and 17, with minor route changes and different callsigns. This intense period of reconnaissance activity scored many new 'firsts' for Det 4 — first occasion that both aircraft were airborne simultaneously, first time KC-10s had been used to refuel SR-71s in the European theatre, first time that photos taken by the SR-71s were released to the press (although the source was never officially admitted and the image quality was purposely severely degraded to hide true capability).

Shutdown

By the late 1980s a powerful constituency of senior Air Force officers and members serving on the Senate's House Permanent Select Committee on Intelligence (HPSCI), made shutdown of the *Senior Crown* programme a personal crusade. By 1988 the protagonists earned a brief reprieve, thereafter however, the antagonists got their way and what was to be the final flight of an SR-71 took place on March 6, 1990, when Ed Yeilding and JT Vida flew '972 on a west to east coast record-breaking flight of the United States, before landing at the Smithsonian National Aerospace Museum, Washington DC, where the aircraft was handed over for permanent display.

Three SR-71As ('962, '967 and '968), were placed in storage at Site 2 Palmdale; two SR-71As ('971 and '980), together with the sole-

surviving SR-71B ('956) were loaned to NASA (see page 80), the remaining 13 aircraft (including the hybrid trainer designated SR-71C, 60-6934), were donated to museums throughout the US, despite more than 40 members of Congress, and many other well-placed officials and senior officers, voicing their concern over the decision.

The Gulf War, provided evidence of a lack of timely reconnaissance material available to General Schwarzkof's field commanders. But it was not until March/April 1994 that events in the international arena once more took a turn. Relations between North Korea and the United States, at best always strained, reached a new low over the North's refusal to allow inspection of their nuclear sites. The campaigning and lobbying paid off as noted in the 'Department of Defence Appropriations Bill 1995' wherein provision was made for a modest, 'three plane SR-71 aircraft contingency reconnaissance capability'.

Of the three SR-71As placed in deep storage at Site 2, Palmdale, only '967 was called to arms. The other 'A' model to be recommissioned was '971 which

had been loaned to NASA, re-numbered '832 and regularly ground tested but never flown by its civilian caretakers eventually to re-enter service with the 9th RW.

The pilot trainer SR-71B, together with the brand new flight simulator, would be shared between the Air Force and NASA, and in a further move to keep operating costs to a minimum the new detachment, designated Det 2, would, like NASA, operate its aircraft from Edwards AFB, California. Since then the political infighting over the future of the SR-71 continued and on October 14, 1997, President Clinton used his line item veto powers to kill $39 million in funding to maintain the two USAF SR-71s. The following day the aircraft were grounded and the Air Force personnel returned to Beale. The Blackbirds operational life was finally over.

At a time when inspection teams are regularly being denied access to a part of the world capable of producing and using on fellow human beings some of the most hideous toxins known to mankind, one may be forgiven for asking if accountants live on the same planet as the rest of us mere mortals. **X**

Above: Blackbird 64-17971 (ex NASA 832) taxies out at Edwards AFB for a Roving Sands sortie in April 1997. Six months later both this and 64-17967 were again retired. (AFM - Steve Fletcher)

Far left: Surviving Blackbirds, including the two-seat SR-71C '981, seen at Beale AFB following the USAF's first termination of SR-71 operations in November 1989. (Lockheed Martin)

Left: Blackbird 64-17967 of the 9th RW's Det 2 at Edwards AFB, seen over the high deserts of California in July 1997 prior to the USAF's second termination of SR-71 operations later that year. (Ted Carlson)

AREA 51

area 51

Right: *Area 51 taken from a Russian satellite in 1991 showing Groom Lake on the right and the Papoose Mountains at the top left behind the main hangar complex. (Photos via Author)*

Below: *A line-up of CIA U-2As wearing NACA logos at Groom Lake, then known as 'The Ranch' in early 1956, was one of the first photographs taken of 'Area 51'*

– No Past – No Future?

L IKE THE SPY who narrates Len Deighton's novels, the US Air Force's secret flight-test base in Nevada appears to go by several different names, none of which can be warranted genuine. In officially declassified documents, it can only be called "a remote location". Geographically, it is Groom Lake. Within the Department of Energy's Nevada Test Site, it is Area 51. Within the Nellis training range, it is *Dreamland*. Those who worked there nicknamed it the 'Ranch', possibly an abbreviation of Kelly Johnson's 'Paradise Ranch' - which was just as satirical as the Central Intelligence Agency's cover name of *Watertown*.

For more than four decades, Area 51 - as good a name as any - has been the most visible portal into the world of 'black' or unacknowledged programmes within the US Department of Defense, the intelligence community and its suppliers. It has grown and changed along with the black world, which was once a small community where the rule-book was the first thing to be shredded, and is now as large and bureaucratic as anything the Pentagon does.

The existence of Area 51 is proof that black projects exist. A secret flight test centre can have only one purpose: to test military aircraft which are visibly different from conventional aircraft, and which embody important military capabilities which can be discerned from their appearance.

Area 51 has had two lives. It was

Bill Sweetman visits America's 'black' test centre that has not 'officially' existed for nearly 45 years.

not created by the US Air Force, but by the CIA. In 1954, the CIA and the Lockheed Skunk Works collaborated to build a reconnaissance aircraft to spy on Russia. It would survive because it would fly above the reach of Soviet air defences, and because it would be developed and operated secretly, so that the Russians would have no time to prepare for it.

Lockheed and the CIA chose Groom Lake as the test site for the new U-2, known by the codename *Aquatone*. The U-2 made its first operational flight in 1956, but by 1958 the aircraft was known to exist, training was relocated to Laughlin, Texas, and the Nevada site saw decreasing use.

Before the U-2 became operational, the CIA set about developing a secret replacement that could continue its mission in the face of improved defences. It was a much more complex and costly programme than the U-2: a bigger aircraft, it used a radical new engine. The hydrogen-fuelled Lockheed CL-400, codenamed *Suntan*, was cancelled before it flew, and its existence was not disclosed for another 20 years.

The CIA immediately started to develop a substitute. In 1959, the Lockheed Skunk Works was chosen to build the Mach 3-plus, hydrocarbon-fuelled A-12,

Above: **The second of two Have Blue stealth technology demonstrators, XST-2 (1002) first flew from Area 51 in June 1978.**

codenamed *Oxcart*. In 1962 the comapany was awarded a contract to build a faster and higher-flying unmanned air vehicle (the D-21, also known as *Tagboard* or *Senior Bowl*), to be launched from a modified A-12.

As the A-12 approached its first flight, which took place in April 1962, Area 51 was expanded and modernised to handle the new spyplane. Although President Lyndon Johnson disclosed the existence of the project in April 1964, the only versions revealed were the experimental YF-12 interceptor, and the heavier SR-71, which replaced the A-12 in mid-1968. The existence of the A-12 and D-21 was secret until 1982.

Meanwhile, the black world expanded into space. In 1960, the Pentagon established the National Reconnaissance Office (NRO) - although, for the next 32 years, it would technically be a felony to admit that it existed. The NRO's mission was to provide space-based intelligence systems to meet the needs of the CIA, the National Security Agency and the armed

forces. As it did so, secret funds amounting to billions of dollars became a permanent feature of the annual USAF budget.

After the CIA's A-12s were retired, Area 51 became home to a growing collection of Soviet aircraft, acquired during the Arab-Israel conflict and by other means. This relatively small operation was the main activity at the base until 1977, when its second life began.

Before that time, everything that went on at Area 51 was connected to the intelligence community, and the base was administered by the CIA and Department of Energy. The spymasters could argue that they were to all intents and purposes at war, and that the traditional ban on secret projects in peacetime did not apply.

It was therefore a very important change in policy when, in early 1976, the Experimental Survivable Testbed (XST) project was taken into the black world, under the codename *Have Blue*. Pentagon decision-makers, led by Dr. William Perry, Carter's under-secretary of defense for research and

engineering, believed that the reductions in radar cross section (RCS) promised by the *Have Blue* programme were so much greater than most of the world believed possible that they had to be protected at all costs.

The *Have Blue* prototypes never flew from any base but Area 51. Its operational follow-on, the F-117A, was also black, and its existence was not disclosed until late 1988, five years after it became operational. The next manned stealth aircraft, Northrop's *Tacit Blue*, remained secret until 1996, 11 years after its flight test programme concluded. Lockheed's first stealth program after the F-117, the *Senior Prom* cruise missile, remains classified.

The idea of secret weapons that could bring down the Soviet Union captivated the new Reagan administration, which took office as Northrop and Lockheed submitted their final proposals for a stealth strategic bomber. The Reaganites wanted to keep the programme in the black world, and made a brief formal announcement only because the project would change Northrop's financial picture beyond all recognition.

Less massive programmes performed by larger companies were not subject to the same considerations. The black budget for both air and space systems boomed, reaching $25 billion per year or more by 1986.

As the secret projects launched in 1981-82 approached the flight-test stage, Area 51 was expanded to accommodate them. It gained new hangars, administrative buildings and a 19,700ft (6,000m) runway, the longest paved runway in the US. Some 90,000 acres of public land to the east of Area 51 were closed off to protect it from observation, and a system of warning devices and patrols, using vehicles and helicopters, was established. Formally, the base fell under the

Right: *Another secret stealth technology aircraft,* Tacit Blue, *remained at Groom Lake from 1982 to 1996 when it was transferred to the Air Force Museum.*

control of the USAF: it is believed to be operated by Detachment 3 of the Air Force Flight Test Center (AFFTC) at Edwards AFB.

In real terms, the US defence budget peaked in 1987. The black budget apparently declined in the late 1980s: however, a closer look showed that its shrinkage was cosmetic, and was due to the fact that large programmes such as the B-2, the F-117, the Navy's A-12 Avenger II and the Advanced Cruise Missile were moving from the black to the white budget. Newer, still-classified projects were thriving.

Many observers expected that the incoming Clinton administration would reduce the black budget through cutbacks and declassification. They were wrong. Clinton's team lost no time in increasing security around the base, closing off more public land to eliminate vantage points which had been discovered in the early 1990s.

A key member of the Clinton defence team was 'the godfather of stealth', Bill Perry, who returned to the Pentagon in 1993, first as deputy secretary of defense and then as secretary. Perry is an advocate of 'silver bullet' forces, able to disrupt an adversary's military operations out of all proportion to its numbers. Silver bullets are not secret by definition, but technological surprise is one of the assets that they bring to a military operation, because it prevents the adversary from developing effective countermeasures.

The black budget has remained healthy. Despite the overall decline in defence expenditures, the USAF's black research and development budget in recent years has been 55-65 per cent higher than it was in the last pre-Clinton budget, for FY1993.

No less than 38 per cent of all USAF spending on hardware - R&D and procurement - is spent on black programmes in the planned FY99 budget. Over three years - FY97-99, representing the maturing of Clinton defence plans - well over $15 billion is to be spent on black R&D in the USAF budget alone, and $21 billion on USAF black-world procurement.

The money is concealed in the budget in a number of ways, some more obvious than others. One section of the R&D budget, Operational Systems Development, includes about 90 line items. Listed expenditures do not add up to the sub-total listed for the section, the $4.5 billion difference comprising most of the USAF's black R&D programmes. Other black

programmes are covered by generic codenames such as Advanced Program Evaluation (more than $1 billion in the Clinton years) and Evaluation and Analysis Program ($450 million).

In the defence industry, the black world has increased in importance. Lockheed Martin's Skunk Works has seldom been larger, despite the fact that its visible output since 1990 comprises two small UAVs. McDonnell Douglas' Phantom Works won substantial business between its foundation in 1992 and the Boeing take-over this year. Boeing's military-aircraft activities - headquartered in a windowless building in Renton - appear to have survived without visible means of support throughout the 1980s.

A useful barometer of activity at Area 51 is the scheduled air service,

using a specially built terminal at Las Vegas airport, which transports staff to the base using Boeing 737s and CT-43s under the call-sign *Janet*. At the most recent count, there appeared to be 12 regular *Janet* flights per day between Las Vegas and the secret base, each capable of carrying more than 120 people. Considering that a major white-world combined test force (CTF) such as the B-2 will involve fewer than 200 people at Edwards, this indicates a high level of activity.

The most recent black aircraft to have been unveiled, Northrop's *Tacit Blue*, had been in storage since 1985, and its origins go back to the Ford Administration. The projects that necessitated the expansion of Area 51 in the mid-1980s and have absorbed tens of billions of dollars are still secret, and

Above: An early operational A-12 Oxcart lands at Area 51 with the Papoose Mountains in the background.
Left: The first YF-12A (60-6934) deploying its large drag 'chute on touch down at Groom Lake after an early test flight in 1963.

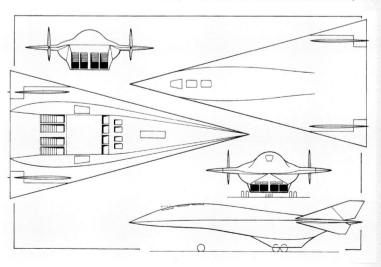

Left: The X-30 National Aero-Space Plane (NASP) project, which was abandoned in 1992, may have been a cover for several USAF 'black' programmes. (Photos via Author)

their identity is a matter of fragmentary reports and educated guesswork.

A consistent series of reports has described flying-wing aircraft in the tactical fighter size class. Several possible projects could account for such sightings: one is a General Dynamics precursor to the A-12, or a Northrop aircraft derived from its Advanced Tactical Aircraft design and closely resembling the B-2.

Lockheed Martin has repeatedly proposed to develop an improved or scaled-up version of the F-117, even in the early days of the programme. Could the company's public marketing be a cover for an aircraft that already exists? Likely improvements would include refined aerodynamics, with a lower sweep angle and smoothed surfaces (the F-117's sharply swept wing and faceting reflected conservative stealth design); more powerful engines (such as the F414 or the A-12's F412); radar (originally planned for the F-117) and a heavier weapon load.

The existence of such an aircraft would explain the retirement of the F-111 and the USAF's lack of enthusiasm for continued production of the B-2A. The largest conflict of the 1990s took place in the Middle East, and it remains one of the world's principal flashpoints. It is a large theatre, and aircraft designed with Central European operations in mind require extensive tanker support to cover it. The longer-ranging F-111 was notably valuable in *Desert Storm*. Without the F-111, the USAF is left with only a smaller-than-planned fleet of F-15Es in the heavy strike role - unless there is a substitute available.

As for the B-2, one suggestion made to the writer - from an informed source - is that the bomber's size and cost is largely set by its ability to penetrate hostile defences to a depth of up to 1,500 miles, spending several hours

within the enemy's air defence net. With the collapse of the Soviet Union, a smaller and less complex aircraft would be adequate.

The codename *Senior Citizen* has been linked in a number of documents to a low-observable, short-take-off and landing transport for special operations. It would be no surprise at all if such an aircraft existed. One of the Pentagon's first plans for extricating US hostages from Tehran in 1980 involved the highly modified, rocket-boosted YMC-130H transport. The final mission failed because there was no aircraft that could fly into Tehran, land in a confined space close to the target and return without refuelling.

Boeing has almost certainly been the prime contractor on a stealth aircraft at some point in time. Otherwise, the Pentagon would object to Lockheed Martin's acquisition of Northrop Grumman, on the grounds that it would create a monopoly of practical stealth experience. One of Boeing's programs may have been the 'Q', a high-altitude, long-endurance stealth reconnaissance aircraft.

The most controversial issue is whether black programmes include hypersonic aircraft, or aerospace vehicles. The question is not whether the US government has sponsored hypersonic research in black programmes, but how much has been done and how far it has progressed.

In the 1960s, many hypersonic technologies were demonstrated in both public and secret ground-test programmes. McDonnell Aircraft designed a Mach 12 vehicle powered by ramjets and rockets. General Dynamics' ramjet-powered Kingfish, rival to the Lockheed A-12, was the subject of wind-tunnel tests after the CIA chose the latter as its U-2 replacement. Marquardt and Pratt & Whitney were both active in propulsion systems. Marquardt's back-lot at Van Nuys houses a 60in (150cm)-diameter rocket-based combined cycle (RBCC) engine (much too large for a missile) developed before 1970, a boron-fuelled ramjet and a Mach 3.8, 20in (50cm) ramjet with a variable inlet and exhaust - all developed for classified projects.

During the 1970s, the USAF's Flight Dynamics Laboratory worked with Lockheed on a hypersonic research aircraft which reached the stage of a full-scale mock-up. A generally authoritative book on Lockheed aircraft, published in 1982, asserted that the company's Skunk Works had flown a research aircraft capable of sustained Mach 6 flight.

In 1982-83, the USAF and industry talked openly about the potential needs and uses for a trans-atmospheric vehicle (TAV), capable of reaching sub orbital altitudes and circling the earth before returning to a standard runway. A classified programme from the early 1980s was *Copper Canyon*, a propulsion study focused on an RBCC engine. It became the starting point for the

X-30 National Aero Space Plane (NASP) project, publicly announced by President Reagan immediately after the Challenger disaster. The stated goal was to demonstrate an air-breathing single-stage-to-orbit (SSTO) vehicle.

Observers were sceptical about the feasibility of the project, intrigued by the tight security surrounding its engine, and puzzled by the fact that Lockheed and McDonnell Douglas had declined to bid on the programme. The USAF denied any black-world links and maintained that NASP was its only high-speed programme, but now admits to the existence of at least three classified SSTO and TAV programmes from the mid-1980s: *Science Dawn*, *Science Realm*, and *Have Region*. None led to flight-test hardware, as far as is known.

Suspicion that NASP was a cover for classified programmes was widespread. Under NASP, the USAF was able to develop manufacturing infrastructure and test facilities to support hypersonics and TAVs, without having to shroud them in Special Access Program (SAP) security rules. Fundamental aerodynamic uncertainties led to the abandonment of NASP in 1992, confirming the doubts of those who had questioned its feasibility all along. Observers would have been even more suspicious had they known about Area 51's new runway. Runway length is largely a function of take-off and landing speed. High take-off and landing speeds result from three design features - short wingspans, high wing loading and low maximum lift coefficient - all of which are combined most commonly in high-supersonic or hypersonic configurations.

Since 1989, there has been a steady flow of eye-witness reports of unusual aircraft, including the sighting of a 75ft delta vehicle over the North Sea and numerous reports from amateur astronomers of 'fast movers' which behave neither like conventional aircraft nor like spacecraft. Since 1991, many US communities have reported 'skyquakes', which have most of the characteristics of a sonic boom from a high-flying aircraft but which cannot be linked to any acknowledged military operation.

Two high-speed vehicles have been reported. One is a high-speed cruise vehicle, flying between Mach 4.5 and Mach 6, which is said to have taken over the mission of the SR-71 (hence the latter's retirement in 1990) with a secondary strike role. The other is a two-stage TAV or

advanced reusable spacecraft.

Interestingly, it has recently been disclosed that the MiG-31M and its Vympel R-37 missile were designed to engage targets cruising at up to Mach 6 and 131,250ft (40000m). Development of this system started in the mid-1980s - at about the same time that the traitor Aldrich Ames began spying for the KGB.

How could such a prominent programme have gone for so long without being compromised in the press? Black projects are developed under Special Access Programs (SAP) restrictions that override normal chains of command, adding a layer of serendipitous disinformation to the security barrier. Gen George Sylvester, commander of Aeronautical Systems Division in 1977, was not 'accessed' into the *Have Blue* programme, even though he was nominally responsible for all USAF aircraft programmes. Had he been asked whether *Have Blue* existed, he could have candidly and honestly denied it.

Sensitive programmes may be developed outside normal channels. The General Atomics RQ-1 Predator exists today because the CIA pursued development of its predecessor, the Gnat 750, in

defiance of a Congressional edict that all UAV programmes should be managed by a single joint programme office.

The odds are against such vehicles being photographed. First of all, there are probably not many of them. After a 20-year programme, the USAF has a single wing of stealth fighters, and a bomber that is not yet operational in a fully capable form. Assuming that black hypersonic programmes started in the early 1980s, it would be surprising if more than a handful of aircraft had been built.

Apparently, a move to declassify the base was quite widely supported during 1996, but was quashed by 'one or two people' at high levels in the Pentagon. It seems absurd that the USAF refuses to acknowledge the existence of a flight-test centre that has been operational for more than 40 years, has been seen and photographed by hundreds (probably thousands) of citizens and described in dozens of magazines and books. Apparently, however, the government feels that the shroud of mystery that surrounds the base, and the myth that it engenders, assists the security system that protects its black projects.

Left: Recently, Boeing 737-200s using the call-sign Janet, one of which is N4539W, seen here on approach to Las Vegas on April 24, 1997, have been making 12 shuttle flights a day between Las Vegas Airport and Area 51. This aircraft, together with five others which were previously operated by the USAF as T-43As, are leased from the Department of the Air Force by EG&G special Projects Inc to operate these flights. (AFM-Steve Fletcher)

Below: The proposed A/F-117X, a carrier-based derivative of the F-117A Nighthawk may already exist at Area 51.

Piotr Butowski reveals some of the more intreging Soviet X-planes, some of which were more successful than others - all of which were 'black'.

Above: *The Soviet Union's most successful reconnaissance aircraft of the Cold War, the MiG-25R, was designed as an interceptor.*

Below: *The remains of Gary Powers U-2 shot down over the Soviet Union in 1960, displayed at Moscow's Central Armed Forces Museum.* (Photos AFM - Archives)

CONTRARY TO APPEARANCES, there has never been a Soviet equivalent of the American U-2! In the late 1950s, when the U-2 penetrated deep into Soviet territory, the Russians were intent on building something like it — indeed, the first U-2 mission on July 4, 1956, when it supposedly flew over Moscow, shocked the Soviet leadership to the core.

On March 1, 1959, flying tests began with the Yak-25RV, a straight wing development of the Yak-25 twin-engined interceptor. The aircraft was built in haste using the existing heavy airframe Consequently, the Yak-25RV's performance never even approached that of the U-2. With a take-off weight of 21,600lb (9,800kg) and wing span of 77ft (23.5m), the practical ceiling of the Yak-25RV amounted to 67,250ft (20,500m), while it had a range of 1,620nm (3,000km). A new wing developed by TsAGI (the Central Aero and Hydrodynamics Institute) would have made it possible to raise the ceiling by 3,250-5,000ft (1,000-1,500m) and increase the range by 20-25%, but it was never fitted.

Although the Yak-25RV was developed as a recce aircraft in response to the American U-2, the roles of the 155 production aircraft made by Factory No.99 in Ulan Ude, were quite different — most became high flying anti-aircraft missile targets! .

Only a few Yak-25RV-Is were used for reconnaissance missions after being converted to Yak-25RRs in 1963. These were tasked with gathering samples of radio-active material following nuclear explosions (RR stands for *radiacyonnaya razvedka* - radiation reconnaissance) and operated along the frontier with China.

It was obvious that the Yak-25RV would never equal the U-2 as a recce aircraft and a completely new design would have to be developed. In the meantime, however, on May 1, 1960, the Soviets were presented with an ideal opportunity — a U-2 had been shot down near Sverdlovsk (now known as Yakaterinburg). The wreckage was thoroughly examined and the order was given to copy it.

The task was assigned to the Beriev's design bureau at Taganrog, and the copy aircraft was to be designated S-13. At the same time, the J75-P13 engine was to be copied in Kazan by Prokophiy Zubet's team under the Russian name RD16-75. A preliminary order was issued for five S-13 aircraft. By March 1961, a full-scale mock-up of the S-13's fuselage had been constructed in metal, but on May 12, 1962 — for undisclosed reasons, the decision was taken to stop all work on the Russian U-2. However, the Soviet aviation industry did benefit from one by-product of the 'red U-2' exercise, namely the V-65

Above: *A wide span Yak-25RV, known in the West as the Flashlight-B, now in the Monino museum.*

RUSSIAN STEALTH

T8-12 is a Su-25 tested with radar absorbing coating.

THE USSR'S FIRST, and perhaps even the world's first stealth aircraft took-off on 25 July 1935.

A group of designers from Moscow's Air Force Academy under direction of Professor S. G. Kozlov, suggested the building an aircraft named PS (*prozrachyi samolot*, transparent aircraft). In order to check the idea they modified a Yak AIR-4 light aircraft by replacing the plywood and canvas skin with French-made 'rodoid' transparent organic glass, while the structural parts, landing gear, etc. were painted with white paint mixed with aluminium powder later covered by 'rodoid' in order to obtain the mirror effect. This solution proved to be effective at the beginning, but after a short period of operation the whole effect was spoiled by small cracks. Upon completion of the AIR-4 experiment, a reconnaissance aircraft was designed using this technology, but was never built.

The problem of reduced radar visibility of aircraft returned in the mid 1970s. Opinions have been expressed that the USSR was unable to build a stealth aircraft because it had no computers powerful enough for such a task - the development of the stealth shape needs enormous numbers of calculations. This is not correct. Russia may be backward with commercial computers, but not with large industrial-military computers It simply did not appreciate the importance of the technology and, although they did some work on it, results were superficial.

The USSR never developed, nor even attempted to develop, an aircraft similar to the F-117. Now low-visibility requirements are taken into consideration for every new aircraft designed in Russia but not to the extent of the F-117 where all other features, particularly the flying handling and performance, were sacrificed for the sake of invisibility. When currently discussing this problem, Russians always emphasise that stealth aircraft have not justified the hopes pinned on them for when observed from several points, as well as with multiple bandwidths (using long-wave stationary surveillance radars), stealth aircraft lose their invisibility.

Russian stealth technology is usually limited to the use of radar absorbing materials and coatings with insignificant interference with the aircraft shape. Attempts at coating aircraft with radiation absorbing layer were carried out in the 1980s with such aircraft as the MiG-23 and Su-25. Once I had an opportunity to touch an Su-25 used for these experiments (the T8-12 prototype). The coating was several millimetres of a thick flexible substance, like hard rubber which would add several hundred kilograms of weight to even a small aircraft.

Local changes in the shape reducing the radar signature may be seen in modern Russian aircraft, such as the flat sharp-edged nose of Su-27IB strike aircraft, the Tu-300 UAV and others. The recently cancelled Mikoyan 1-42 fighter carries its weapons in an internal armament bay, while the Sukhoi S-37 fighter uses a conformal weapons container under the fuselage.

Russians are also working on other ways of obtaining 'invisibility' by generating a sort of electronic force field around the aircraft, but little information about this is available.

The Su-27IB's (Su-32FN) flat nose gives some stealth features.
(Photos Piotr Butowski)

steel alloy developed following analysis of the U-2 wreck.

The Myasishchev M-17 made its maiden flight on May 26, 1982, — 20 years after the U-2 piloted by Francis Gary Powers was shot down. It might have seemed that the new design was intended to fulfil the same role as the U-2 — a high-altitude reconnaissance aircraft — but it was not... This aircraft had been developed to shoot down balloons! At the design stage, the M-17 had faced a rival in the shape of the Yak-25PA (*perekhvatchik aerostatov* - balloon interceptor), a variant of the Yak-25RV armed with a movable 23mm cannon. Reconnaissance balloons drifting at high altitudes were very troublesome to the USSR. These aerostats were regularly sent over Warsaw Pact countries between 1956 and 1977, after which they were seen less often (except for short bursts of activity, for instance in December 1980 as Warsaw Pact armies prepared to intervene in Poland). Of the 4,112 balloons detected over USSR territory, 793 were shot down. When the M-17 was spotted at Ramenskoye (Zhukovsky) airfield by a US satellite it was given a temporary code-name, *Ram-M* which was later changed to *Mystic-A*.

The M-17 is a twin-boom aircraft with a single RD36-51V turbojet engine installed in the rear part of a short fuselage. The aircraft was intended to climb quickly to a high altitude (unlike the U-2 which had a slow rate of climb), but the flight duration was only 1.5-2 hours compared with the U-2's 10 hours plus. An armament system for the M-17 was planned and tested on a Tu-16, but never installed.

By the late 1980s, the balloon interceptor was no longer needed but in the meantime, the armed forces had found another task for the high-altitude aircraft: reconnaissance and target indication for tactical missiles and strike aircraft. The two existing M-17s were used in a test programme prior to the design and construction of the new variant.

This was intended to become part of the *Proriv* (Break) reconnaissance-strike system designed to attack small fixed and movable targets behind enemy lines such as radar sites, command posts and missile launchers. The aircraft would be able to observe enemy movements from a high altitude several dozen kilometres inside its own territory. The reconnaissance data was transmitted by radio to a ground command post and then on to strike commands. Thanks to real-time data transmissions, targets could be hit with an accuracy of several metres. This system is comparable to the American Assault Breaker or PLSS (Precision Location Strike System).

To fulfil this new role, the M-17's performance requirements were changed. A very high ceiling became less important but duration was now crucial. The aircraft had to observe the battlefield for many hours while carrying 4,000lb (1,800kg) of special electronic equipment (the M-17's armament only weighed 500lb [230kg]). The new aircraft was designated M-55 by the Myasishchev team, while the armed forces, considering it to be a modification of the former model, named it M-17RM (*razvedchik modi-fitsirovannyi* - modified reconnaissance aircraft). The first prototype was flown by Eduard Cheltsov on September 16, 1988. The NATO code-name for this aircraft was *Mystic-B*.

The most important development in the aircraft's design was a new powerplant consisting of two D-30V12 turbofans. The higher total take-off thrust meant that the fuel reserve and duration of flight could be increased — at 12 miles (20,000m) altitude the M-55 can fly for 4 hours 12 minutes or for 5 hours at 10 miles (17,000m).

At least five M-55s have been built to date, but a lack of funding has halted production at the Smolensk factory even though the Russian Air Force still has great interest in the type. Some reports have stated that two aircraft are currently being tested by the military.

Supercruise reconnaissance.

There have been several attempts by the Soviet Union to construct strategic reconnaissance aircraft with a supersonic cruising speed. In March 1954, Pavel Tsybin submitted a proposal for an ultra-modern strategic RS (*reaktivnyi samolot* - jet aircraft) bomber capable of delivering a nuclear bomb at a distance of 8,700 miles (14,000km) flying at an altitude of 18.6 miles (30,000m) and a speed of 1,865 mph (3,000km/h). The RS was to be very small, its take-off weight was not to exceed 22 tons, and two ramjet engines were to be installed at the tips of very thin trapezoid wings. The assumed weight of the structure was only 22% of the take-off weight, while the fuel weight was to amount to 75%. However, in the course of detailed design work, it quickly became obvious that the theory did not work and there was no way of putting it into practice with the available technology.

For the next design the structural weight was assumed, more realistically, to be 43% of the take-off weight, whereas the range was reduced by half— but there were still more changes to come. The problems associated with the RS went from bad to worse — while the design performances were constantly reduced. Eventually in August, 1956, it was decided to construct a reconnaissance version named RSR (the second R stands for *razvedchik* - reconnaissance) with an operational radius of 1,050 miles (1,700km), a spped of 1,430mph (2,800km/h) and a ceiling of 87,600ft (26,700m).

On April 7 1959, Amet-Khan Sultan made the first flight with the NM-1 (*naturnyi maket*, demonstrator) RSR aircraft which was smaller and powered by less powerful AM-5 turbojets. In 1959-1960, the NM-1 made 32 flights at altitude of 13,125ft (4,000m) a speed of 305mph (490 km/h). In 1959, production of a preliminary series of the RSR (called R-020) was started at the Ulan-Ude plant. None were ever flown, however, although three were ready when work was stopped in the spring of 1961.

One of the reasons of Tsybin's failure was competition from Andrei Tupolev who was then developing a pilotless strategic reconnaissance vehicle named the Tu-123 *Yastreb* (Hawk). In May 1964, the *Yastreb* entered service and later the Voronezh factory produced 52 of the delta winged drone powered by single Tumansky KR-15 turbojet engine. Equipment included four cameras and the *Romb* (Rhombus) ELINT unit. The Tu-123's take-off weight was 84,875lb (38,500kg) including 36,600lb (16,600kg) of fuel. The cruising speed was 2,800 km/h (Mach 2.55) at an altitude of 21-22 km of altitude, with a range 2,230miles (3,600km).

Despite rumours about *Yastrebs* taking-off from Belorus to perform reconnaissance missions along the coasts of European NATO countries, and over China, only flights at training ranges in the depths of Soviet Union were made.

The *Yastreb* was very expensive since it was a single use device (only the nose carrying the recce pack could be recovered) similar to that of Lockheed's D-21, and its cost was similar to that of a normal aircraft. A prototype Tu-139 *Yastreb-2* , all of which could be recovered by parachute, was flight tested in July 1968 but not put into production. Following the introduction of the MiG-25R in 1972, *Yastrebs* were gradually withdrawn from service.

Foxbat
The Soviet Union's most successful

Left: The steep take-off of the Myasishchev M-17 Mystic-A balloon interceptor.

Above: A Tu-16 test bed with an M-17 nose and gun camera turret above the fuselage. (Dave Allport)

Left: The M-55 (M-17RM) has been ordered by the Russian Air Force as a compo-nent of its recon-naissance-strike system. (Author)

'spyplane' was the MiG-25 *Foxbat*, an aircraft originally overestimated by the West but underestimated now. It was designed in the mid 1960s as a defence against US Mach 3 aircraft then under development - the XB-70 and SR-71, as well as the AGM-28 Hound Dog cruise missile. Almost two thirds of the 1,186 MiG-25 aircraft manufactured were fighters, but only the reconnaissance version survived the test of time and is still used in Russia today.

In spite of its unconventional design, the MiG-25 was a much more orthodox aircraft than the SR-71 and therefore built in much greater numbers. At first, in view of its designed 1,550mph (2,500 km/h) cruising speed, a titanium structure was considered. Although expensive, it was the difficulties of using titanium alloys that dictated that steel remained the main structural material. Eventually the MiG-25 was made of 80% steel, 8% titanium alloys and 11% aluminium. Due to the high operating temperatures, multiple stage cooling systems were necessary to ensure acceptable conditions for the pilot and the on-board equipment. With a maximum take-off weight of 90,830lb (41,200kg), the MiG-25 is capable of cruising at 2,500 km/h (Mach 2.35) carying a full bomb load. The MiG-25 is powered by two R-15B-300 turbojets, as used in the *Yastreb*. As they are adapted for a supersonic cruising speed the aircraft's range is similar at supersonic and subsonic speeds (1,015miles (1,635km) and 1,150 miles (1,865km) respectively, or 1,325 miles (2,130km) and 1,490 miles (2,400km) with additional fuel tanks). New equipment in the MiG-25 included the TsVM-10-155 Orbita digital computer for accurate bombing at Mach 2.35 from an

altitude of 65,500ft (20,000m).

The maiden flight of the *Foxbat* prototype, E-155R-1, was made on March 6, 1964 with Alexander Fedotov at the controls, and the MiG-25R reconnaissance aircraft entered service in December 1972. However, the combat debut of the MiG-25R took place even before its official commissioning into Soviet fighter units.

On March 21, 1971 Soviet An-22 heavy transports landed at Cairo West airfield in great secrecy with four MiG-25Rs in their holds. From October 1971 to March 1972 the aircraft flew reconnaissance missions from Egypt over the Mediterranean, the Sinai Peninsula and Israeli territory. The MiG-25Rs left Egypt on June 6, 1972, only to return again from October 19, 1973 to June 1974. On this occasion the four *Foxbats* were the MiG-25RBV version.

Only Soviet pilots flew the MiG-25 in Egypt, the Egyptians were not permitted to get close to the aircraft. At first the Soviet pilots flew training reconnaissance missions over Egyptian territory. They later flew over Israeli territory at a height of 65,500ft (20,000m). The unarmed MiG-25R was protected during take-off and landing by MiG-21 fighters but several minutes after take-off the *Foxbat* accelerated to Mach 2.35 and protection was no longer needed. No MiG-25 was lost operating from Egypt.

The covert use of the MiG-25 in Egypt required sophisticated backup. The aircraft were fitted with self-destruct devices in the event of an Israeli landing. Also, emergency routes back to Soviet territory were prepared during which they would be escorted by Soviet fighters and air defence

elements of the Soviet Navy, routes which inevitably violated the air space of other countries. The MiG-25R was in production for a very short time before being replaced by the dual-role MiG-25RB (reconnaissance/bomber) in 1970 which was capable of carrying four 1,100lb (500kg) bombs or a single nuclear weapon. Later, after changing the underwing pylons, the MiG-25RB could carry up to 11,00lb (5,000kg) of bombs.

Reconnaissance equipment of the MiG-25RB included three cameras and the Romb ELINT system which was later replaced by the new *Virazh* (Turn) in the MiG-25RBV, and eventually with the *Tangazh* (Pitch) unit in the MiG-25RBT. Eight MiG-25RBVs were also equipped with radiation reconnaissance equipment and took over the China border patrol from the Yak-25RRs monitoring Chinese nuclear tests.

More specialised variants were the MiG-25RBK equipped with the more powerful *Kub* (Cube) ELINT system, and the MiG-25RBS with *Sabla* (Sword) side-looking airborne radar (SLAR), both without cameras. The *Kub* system was later replaced with the *Shar* (Sphere) thus creating the MiG-25RBF, while the *Sabla* SLAR in the RBS was replaced by the *Shompol* (Ramrod) radar thus creating the MiG-25RBSh. All the modifications of the MiG-25RB are covered by only two NATO codenames: *Foxbat-B* for aircraft equipped with cameras or *Foxbat-D* for aircraft with electronic equipment only. As the MiG-25 started its flight tests, the Soviets began the design of a much heavier Mach 3 reconnaissance bomber with a range of 3,725 miles (6,000km). From Sukhoi, Tupolev and Yakovlev designs, the Sukhoi T-

Left: The unmanned Yastreb was powered by single KR-15 turbojet giving it a cruising speed of Mach 2.55. (Photos via Author)

4 was chosen with the prototype flying on August 22, 1972 piloted by Vladimir Ilyushin. Due to its projected maximum speed, the basic structural material had to be titanium. The T-4 had an empty weight of 55 tonns, normal take-off weight of 128 tonnes, and a maximum take-off weight of 136 tonnes. Powered by four RD36-41 turbojets the aircraft had to reach a maximum speed of 2,000mph (3,200km/h) and cruise at 1,860mph (3,000km/h) at an altitude of 65,600-78,750ft (20-24,000m).

The T-4 prototype made only ten flights, the last on January 22, 1974, only one of which was supersonic . In 1975, Pavel Sukhoi decided to stop work on the T-4 and the prototype was handed over to the Monino museum while three more in various stages of construction were scrapped.

Red Aurora.

The name *Aurora* should not be applied to to an American project but to the Soviet Union's most advanced 'black' programme. The

gunshot that began the October Revolution was fired from the cruiser *Aurora* was it not? The Soviets started work on hypersonics soon after the first space flight of Yuriy Gagarin, mainly for military aerospace systems. In the 1960s, the TsAGI institute began research on long duration flights of piloted aircraft in the atmosphere with speeds of up to Mach 4-5, as well as on short-flight space vehicles entering the atmosphere at speeds of Mach 2.5-3. The first such system was the Mikoyan Spiral vehicle, a two-stage vehicle with a hypersonic carrier aircraft which accelerated to Mach 6 at an altitude of 98,500ft (30,000m) carrying a detachable piloted orbital aircraft EPOS (Experimental Piloted Orbital aircraft - both the stages were designated *izdeliye* 50 and the whole system was named *izdeliye* 50-50). The main purpose of the orbital aircraft was to destroy other space vehicles, while other versions were intended for reconnaissance or even bombing.

Work on Spiral was begun in 1965

Below: The legendary Mach 3 Sukhoi T-4, theatre bomber and reconnaissance aircraft, flown in 1972, is seen here on display at the Monino museum. (Dave Allport)

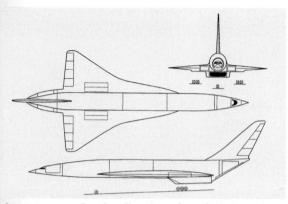

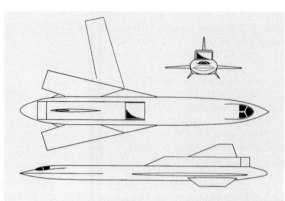

Right: *Drawing of the Mikoyan 301 hypersonic strike and reconnaissance aircraft.*

Far Right: *Drawing of the Tupolev Mach 6 bomber developed from the Tu-2000 project.*

Below right: *The Mikoyan 105-11 test bed for landing trials of the EPOS orbital vehicle was flown in 1976-1978.*

Below: *A model of the 50-50 Spiral aerospace system with Mach 6 carrier and the small piloted orbital combat aircraft.*

by a team under the direction of Gleb Lozino-Lozinsky, Artiom Mikoyan's deputy, and they concentrated on EPOS, three prototypes of which were to be built: 105-11 for subsonic tests with 105-12 and 105-13 for space tests. Only 105-11 was built, after several short hops, made its first flight on October 11, 1976 with Aviard Fastovets at the controls. A year later, the vehicle was launched for the first time from a Tu-95K carrier at an altitude of 16,500ft (5,000m) and landed on a ground airstrip. During successive months 105-11 made eight flights, but in September 1978 the flights were stopped after it suffered damage during landing. In February 1976, in answer to the US Space Shuttle programme, the Soviets decided on the construction of a similar Energia/Buran system and the Spiral programme was gradually abandoned.

At end of the 1970s attention was switched to 'normal' hypersonic aircraft, having nothing in common with space systems. The Soviet air force issued a requirement for hypersonic reconnaissance and bomber aircraft but neither the air force or designers had a clear idea

of what exact requirements were to be met by a hypersonic aircraft. Therefore work was continued in two ways. The first, making use of existing technology, was the construction of an Mach 4-4.5 aircraft made of conventional materials and powered by jet engines. As expected, this path was followed by the Mikoyan team which had more experience of producing supersonic aircraft than any other company in the world (they built over 1,500 MiG-25 and MiG-31 aircraft capable of cruising at Mach 2.35, whereas all the remaining manufacturers in the world had built only a few dozen aircraft such as the SR-71, Tu-144 and Concorde).

The hypersonic Mikoyan 301 was designed as a steel welded structure powered by two turbo-ramjet engines, operating as normal turbofans below Mach 3.5 and as ramjets above that speed. Cruising speed was to be 4,250 km/h (Mach 4) at an altitude of 82-88,000ft (25-27,000m). The designed take-off weight was about 80 tonnes, half of which was the fuel. The fuselage was long and flat, and in order to operate from existing airfields, it had variable geometry wings. Two

variants of 301 were to be used, a reconnaissance aircraft equipped with ELINT and SLAR, and a bomber with stand-off missiles carried internally. The 301 programme was considered a priority by the air force but since the break-up of the Soviet Union it remains on the drawing board.

The second method of constructing a hypersonic aircraft went beyond Mach 5. The limiting factor is the type of fuel. The maximum speed which may be obtained with jet fuel is Mach 4-5. Above this speed cryogenic fuels, liquid hydrogen or methane are more efficient. Also a new airfield infrastructure was necessary. The task of designing a Mach 6 aircraft was taken up by the Tupolev Design Bureau which began work on a heavy hypersonic bomber in 1986. Initially they intend to develop a relatively small Mach 6 experimental aircraft, the Tu-2000A with a length of 180-200ft (55-60m), a wingspan of 46ft (14m) and a maximum weight of 70-90 tonnes. The work done before funds were stopped in 1992 included the construction of a nickel alloy wing torque box, some elements of the fuselage as well as

Above: *Yakovlev's projected high-altitude endurance UAV, code named* Oriol. *(Photos Author)*

the tank for cryogenic fuel and fuel pipes of a unique composite material. The aircraft was to be powered by a group of variable-cycle turbojet/ramjet engines fuelled with liquid hydrogen.

The experience with the Tu-2000A was intended to be used for construction of three other aircraft, two Mach 6 bombers and an airliner. The bomber would have an empty weight of 200 tonnes, take-off weight of 350 tonnes, a length of 330ft (100m), a wing span of 133ft (40.7m), and lifting surface of 1,250m². Six liquid-hydrogen engines would propel the aircraft to Mach 6 at an altitude of 99,000ft (30,000m), with a range of 5,500-6,250 miles (9-10,000km). The crew would consist of two pilots and its weapons would be carried in two wing-root bays. Tupolev also intends to build a single-stage space vehicle weighing 260 tons with a speed of Mach 25 capable of delivering an 8-10 ton bomb load from a 125 mile (200km) orbit. The power pack will include eight ramjets plus supersonic combustion speed or liquid-fuel rocket engines. During 1980s, the Yakovlev Design

Bureau also worked on a military hypersonic aircraft but no information about this design is available.

Yakovlev was also involved with Russia's strategic unmanned reconnaissance vehicle (UAV) programme named *Oriol* (Eagle). This is designed for radar reconnaissance and early warning, an equivalent of the US Global Hawk High Altitude Endurance UAV, able to fly for 24 hours or more at an altitude of over 65,000ft (20,000m). Yakovlev, Myasishchev and Tupolev all submitted designs for the *Oriol* programme. The vehicle designed by Yakovlev had a span of more than 100ft (30m), a take-off weight of 4,410lb (2,000kg) with a turbo-diesel engine driving a 20ft (6m) diameter propeller. The reconnaissance sensor was a phased-array SLAR installed along the fuselage.

The most advanced *Oriol* UAV design came from the Myasishchev team with a twin-boom configuration similar to its M-60 high-altitude aircraft. However, work on *Oriol* has been stopped by lack of funds.

PAINTING TRICKS

Above: The first prototype of the Ka-50 had a dummy second cockpit and small transport cabin window painted on the fuselage.

Now, after discussing super aircraft and hyper speeds, something to laugh at. Who will guess which Russian aircraft (among those in service) was kept secret for the longest time? It was the Ka-50 helicopter.

Its maiden flight took place in 1982 and it was ten years before Sergei Mikheyev presented it during a fighter helicopter conference in London (without even giving the helicopter a name!) in January 1992.

Why was the Ka-50 kept secret for such a long time when other Soviet aircraft were disclosed as a result of Gorbachev's *glasnost* policy?

It was because the Ka-50 was quite different from other combat helicopters: It is the only helicopter with a single pilot and this fact was disguised by painting a false second cockpit, as well as a small transport cabin window, on the prototype! Similar tricks were applied to the Su-25T prototype (by painting a false second cockpit) and with the MiG-29M (by painting non-existing air intakes in the wing roots). MiG-25BM air-defence suppression fighters in operational units were also 'offically' disguised as MiG-25P fighters.

Above: Non-existent air intakes painted on the wing roots of a MiG-29 Fulcrum. (Photos Author)
Below: Thanks to typical air-defence painting this MiG-25BM strike aircraft looks like a MiG-25P interceptor. (Alexei Mikheyev)

Jon Lake reports on the F-117A 'Black Jet' at war.

THE USAF ONLY ever received 59 F-117As, barely sufficient to equip a single, under-strength wing, and the number of aircraft available has subsequently been reduced by attrition. But despite the small number of aircraft involved in the programme, the F-117A is today arguably the most significant aircraft type in the USAF inventory, and is widely regarded as being the 'aircraft which won the Gulf War'. The accuracy figures claimed for the F-117A during Operation *Desert Storm* have been disputed since the end of the war, and critics have pointed out limitations and constraints affecting the aircraft. But no-one can dispute the fact that not one F-117 was lost to the intense AAA and barrages of SAMs encountered over their assigned targets in Iraq. And these were targets which were so heavily defended that the F-117A was the only manned aircraft assigned to attack them.

The F-117 began life as Project *Senior Trend*, a strike fighter development of the stealth technology demonstrator, *Have Blue*. Once it became clear that DARPA's original 'Radar Camouflage' project could result in an operational stealth aircraft, the programme moved into the intense secrecy of the so-called 'Black World'. As Lockheed's famous Skunk Works' was commissioned to design and build a Stealth Fighter, it was decided that even the existence of the aircraft would be a closely-guarded secret.

This was appropriate since the aircraft was not seen as being a mainstream type, to equip mainstream frontline units, and

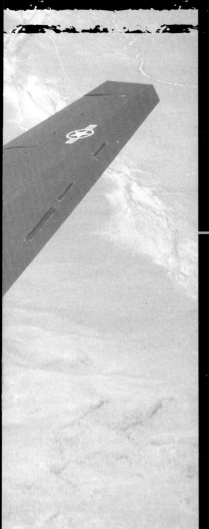

Left: *Night Hawk 85-0816 took part in Operation Desert Storm flying from Khamis Mushait Air Base in Saudi Arabia. (Lockheed Martin)*

operating openly as it does now. Instead the aircraft was seen as an airborne equivalent to the US Army's Special Forces or to Navy SEALs, with a secretive, covert role. The F-117A would be a 'smokeless gun', able to attack terrorist targets or rogue nations on the direct orders of the President, without exposing their identity or origin. F-117A's operated under a concept known as 'Plausible Deniability', under which the President or government could deny the participation of US forces in a particular attack. It was originally expected that only a single squadron would be acquired, and that this would perhaps be manned and administered by the

CIA, as the first U-2s had been." This tiny 'Silver Bullet' force would almost certainly have remained based at Groom Lake (home to the flight test team), but Congress (or those parts of Congress aware of the programme) pressed for a Wing-strength unit, and this necessitated finding a larger base for the type.

Existing USAF bases were too well-known and too accessible, and so a remote disused airfield (Tonopah) in the Nellis AFB range complex was re-activated. A new unit, the 4450th Tactical Group, was formed, and began receiving its aircraft from August 1982. The unit achieved its Initial Operating Capability in October 1983, by which time 14 aircraft had been delivered. The use of F-117As was integrated into USAF war-planning, as a means of attacking the most heavily defended targets with precision, and without being detected. Plans like 'Downshift 02', for example, envisaged the aircraft being used to attack the dacha of the Soviet President in the event of a war between the Superpowers. But the aircraft was primarily intended for use in more 'limited war' scenarios.

From October 1983, two aircraft were maintained on two-hour alert, and as soon as sufficient aircraft were available some 12 aircraft were assigned to stand-by duties. There was a degree of hesitation in actually using the F-117A 'for real'. Many senior officers new nothing of the type's existence, let alone its capabilities, and so 'requests from the customer' were not received. Others doubted whether the aircraft was really ready, and some were unwilling to use the aircraft for fear of compromising secrecy.

During the very month that the

aircraft attained its IOC, there were suggestions that it might be used in support of Operation *Urgent Fury* — the US invasion of Panama, and during the same month preparations were made for an attack by between five and ten F-117As against PLO targets in the Lebanon. The aircraft allocated to the mission had their INS sets fully aligned, and pilots arranged to fly to Myrtle Beach to refuel and undertake a face-to-face brief with their tanker crews, and the pilots of what were optimistically referred to as 'other support aircraft'. The mission was cancelled 45 minutes before the planned take-off time. Also during 1983 Colonel Oliver North planned an F-117A attack against Colonel Gaddafi, with NAS Rota in Spain selected as the 'jumping off point'. This mission too was cancelled at the last moment, perhaps as a result of Spanish objections.

F-117As were readied for action against Libya again, in April 1986, when the type was selected for participation in Operation *El Dorado Canyon*, the US air strikes against Benghazi and Tripoli, eventually carried out by British-based F-111s and carrier-based US Navy aircraft.

The F-117A finally emerged from the 'Black World' on November 10, 1988, when the Pentagon released a single photo of the aircraft. .

With its aircraft in the open, the 4450th Tactical Group adopted the traditions and identity of the 37th Fighter Wing on October 5, 1989, though it remained at the highly secure base at Tonopah.

Some weeks later, on December 19, 1989, the new unit finally took the USAF's enigmatic 'Black Jet' to war. Six F-117As took off from Tonopah and headed south, soon hooking up

Above: *A Paveway III laser-guided bomb (LGB) being dropped from one of the twin internal weapons bays of F-117A 85-0794. Note the faceted ends of the bomb bay door. (Lockheed Martin)*

Right: *A ground crewman checks a GBU-27A/B 2,000lb Paveway III LGB in the weapons bay of an F-117A.*

Below: *F-117A Night HAwk 85-0823 of the 49th FW/9th FS The Flying Nights based at Holloman AFB, New Mexico (Artwork Pete West)*

with their tankers. Two of the aircraft had been assigned to the support of Special Forces troops tasked with capturing Panama's leader, General Noriega, and had their mission cancelled when it became clear that the General had vanished. Confusion surrounds the mission flown by the remaining pair of aircraft. The offical line is that they intended to bomb an empty field to divert attention from a parachute landing by Ranger Battalions. Some questioned whether the stealthiness and accuracy provided by the F-117A was necessary to ensure the success of a mission whose modest aim was to hit a massive field, and to miss a pair of buildings. Others suggested that the primary reason for using the F-117A was to allow Congress to see some visible return from the weapon which they now knew about, and which they had 'unwittingly' funded for so long. Unfortunately, the raid revealed more about the F-117A's weaknesses than about its

strengths. In the absence of clear briefings to the contrary many assumed that the F-117As had failed to hit the barracks blocks, which had been wrongly taken to have been the targets.

The official explanation was that a last-minute change in orders caused the first aircraft to bomb wide, and that the second aircraft's aim-point was an offset from the first bomb, and not a fixed point on the ground. When the first aircraft missed its target, it was thus inevitable that the second aircraft would also miss. In fact, it soon became apparent that the F-117A's IRADS sensor had performed poorly in the high humidity, and that the vegetation lowered IR contrast to an unacceptably low level.

At the end of the day, the raid was judged to have been a success by those who mattered — the customers — the Rangers themselves, who judged that the bombs had caused enough confusion to save lives on both sides. But whether Congress was

convinced by the demonstration remains open to doubt. Fortunately, the next combat use of the F-117A was decisive enough to convince any sceptics.

When the International Community decided to act to force Iraq to withdraw from Kuwait, it was necessary to mount a heavy, but limited offensive against Iraq's military and command infrastructure, minimising human casualties and collateral damage on both sides. The aim was to tear out the eyes, ears, and heart of Iraq's military machine swiftly and at minimum cost. The proposed military campaign demanded speed and surgical precision, and a high percentage of the most important targets were in or around Baghdad, where AAA and SAMs would make attacks by conventional aircraft extremely dangerous and costly. Thus when General Chuck Horner planned his co-ordinated air campaign against Iraq, he placed a heavy reliance on the F-117A, which he believed could operate over Baghdad with complete impunity.

History was to prove him correct, though most Stealth Fighter pilots could not believe that their aircraft could all return home safely in the face of the awesome barrage of flak and SAMs thrown up against them, even if the weapons were being fired without guidance. It was a gamble, though, staking all on the F-117A's technology working as advertised. In case it did not, there were complex plans to bomb the wreckage of any downed Stealth Fighter, to prevent its secrets from being compromised.

The 415th TFS, with 22 F-117As, deployed to Khamis Mushayt in Saudi Arabia, leaving Tonopah on August 19, 1990, night-stopping at Langley AFB. Khamis Mushayt was very similar to Tonopah in many respects, lying at a similar elevation in similar desert terrain. Some called it 'Tonopah East'. The second frontline squadron (the 416th TFS) was deployed to Khamis in December 1991, as it became clear that Saddam Hussein would not back down, and that more F-117As might be required. The deployment of these aircraft threatened to over-stretch the F-117A's traditional tankers (the KC-

135s of the 'Beale Bandits', who had been the only unit cleared to refuel the F-117As during the 'Black World' days). The Beale-based tankers were thus joined by KC-135Rs from an AFRes unit from Grissom AFB, Indiana, although when war began, a wider pool of tanker units supported the Stealth Fighters. Only a handful of aircraft was left behind at Tonopah with the 417th TFTS.

Two waves of F-117As were launched on the night of January 16/17, 1991, the opening night of *Desert Storm*. These were led by Lt Col Ralph Getchell, the 415th's CO, and Al Whitley, CO of the 37th TFW and de facto detachment commander. Several of the pilots had flown combat missions over Vietnam, and none had experienced anything like the barrage of fire thrown up over Baghdad. Several expected to be the sole survivor of the night's raids, yet not one aircraft was even touched.

On that (and subsequent) nights, the F-117As generally flew with two 2,000lb (900kg) bombs each, and each usually attacked two targets. Captain Marcel Kerdavid won a Silver Star for his attacks on the 370ft (112m) Al Quark communications relay tower and on the National Command Alternate Bunker. Sometimes one F-117A would punch an initial hole in a building's roof, and a subsequent aircraft would drop a second bomb through the resulting aperture. The F-117As represented only 2.5% of the first night 'shooters', yet hit 31% of the first night targets. The F-117As actually ran out of strategic targets, and were quickly assigned to attacks on tactical targets like hardened aircraft shelters. The force flew 1,271 sorties during the

Left: *F-117A 85-0812 of the 49th FW flying with a Royal Nether-lands Air Force F-16A during one of Night Hawk's rare European deployments. (RNAF)*

war (about 6,900 flying hours) and carried 2,567 bombs to their targets. In all, 1,669 were assessed as scoring direct hits, 418 were rated as 'misses' and 480 were 'no drops' as a result of poor weather.

And since Operation *Desert Storm*, F-117As have been a regular fixture in Saudi Arabia, and later Kuwait, available to mount attacks against Baghdad or against the Presidential Palaces of Saddam Hussein if the Iraqi regime steps out of line or continues to ignore its obligations to the UN, imposed when the war ended. On January 13, 1993, six F-117As (each with a single bomb) attacked SAM sites and operations centres in Iraq. Low cloud caused broken laser locks on the aircraft attacking SAM sites, and not one of the four bombs hit their targets. Weather prevented another aircraft from finding its target, but the sixth aircraft bombed successfully. F-117A missions have almost certainly been planned in other parts of the world too, perhaps targeting war criminals in the former Yugoslavia, or terrorist training camps in the Middle East.

However, the aircraft is not in any sense a miraculous answer to any air power problem. Initial accuracy claims in the order of 80% have been dramatically down-graded, and it now seems that the F-117A is no more accurate than any other major autonomous LGB platform, and may even be slightly less accurate than aircraft like the TIALD-equipped Jaguar. Moreover, the use of LGBs is by no means a universal panacea, and there are many circumstances in which laser and electro-optically guided weapons cannot be used.

The F-117A's IR-reliant weapons system performs well in the southwestern USA, in desert states like Arizona, New Mexico, Utah and Nevada, but has serious problems in humid climates, or in the presence of any low cloud, dust-storms or even smoke. Even in Iraq, many F-117A missions were aborted because of poor weather, and on some nights, missions could not be mounted at all. It can be imagined that in a West European winter (for example) the F-117A would seldom be able to operate with any degree of reliability or consistency. Moreover, there are worrying doubts as to the ability of the aircraft's RAM-covered surface to retain its 'stealthiness' when wet, and that the material is actually damaged by rain. Even in the southwestern USA, F-117As have to be kept undercover when not flying. How successful the F-117A would be if used over the former Yugoslavia remains open to question.

Congress pressed the USAF to buy 24 more F-117As instead of extra F-16Cs, but this was strongly resisted. To a certain extent, the F-117A was a victim of its own success, since some believed that its very success might threaten future procurement of JSF or JAST, or other future air-to-ground platforms. Others, such as General Buster Glossom, had genuine complaints. He charged that the F-117A was "archaic, 15-year-old technology" that was "a nightmare to maintain".

Left: The *Night Hawk* pilot's view of the world encased in his late 1970s-era cockpit. (Lockheed Martin)

SPIRITS I
s p i r i t s s i

THE SKY

Project Senior CJ

Bob Archer traces the Northrop B-2A stealth bomber's journey from Cold War 'Black' to New World Order 'Blue'.

THE FIRST NORTHROP B-2A Spirit was rolled out of Plant 42 at Palmdale, California on November 22, 1988. The ceremony was carefully orchestrated by Northrop to prevent the 500 invited guests from gaining a glimpse of the aircraft's revolutionary wing design, as all those present were afforded only a front view from ground level. However, Northrop had failed to restrict the airspace overhead resulting in the US journal *Aviation Week and Space Technology* obtaining some spectacular photographs from a hired Cessna! Up until that time the aircraft had, in effect, been a 'black' project, although its unveiling to the press and dignitaries lifted the cloak of secrecy to a degree, and enabled the world's first stealth bomber to commence the long road to operational status. Like the F-117A 'stealth' fighter, the B-2A has enjoyed a unique security cordon wherever and whenever either type has been placed on public view, normally involving armed guards and two rings of barriers, all designed to add to the hype.

The B-2 design was simply a flying wing with virtually no other conventional components. The concept, although radical, was not new, as 'Jack' Northrop, founder of the company, had built the XB-35 with no fuselage commencing in 1940. Powered by four propeller-driven engines, the design was not meant to be stealthy. The advent of the new jet engine era forced a redesign, with Northrop contracted to build two YB-49s, which were essentially similar to the XB-35, but were powered by eight Allison turbojets. Despite an accident to the second of these in January 1948, the USAF ordered 30 RB-49A reconnaissance versions, although budget cuts to several programmes, including the flying wing, ended a potentially promising design.

The advent of low observability (simplified as LO), known universally as 'stealth', led some of the major aerospace manufacturers in the United States to adopt the concept as a method of producing aircraft which could evade detection by radar. Lockheed was one company whose Advanced Development Projects (ADP) section produced the Have Blue stealth design which led to the highly successful F-117A Night Hawk. However, the Air Force required low observability to be extended beyond that of fighters, as the need for a deep penetration bomber with stealth characteristics was given a high priority. The B-1A was under development by Rockwell, and despite showing potential, had been overtaken by events in the spectrum of low observability. Not surprisingly, President Jimmy Carter cancelled the B-1A, ostensibly due to budgetary

Main Picture: Looking unlike any other aircraft, the B-2A Spirit. (Ted Carlson)

Left: Two B-2s were seen together for the first time in the early 1990s on the Palmdale ramp at dusk.

Above: The B-2A Spirit flies in a formation with an Air Combat Command B-52H Stratofortress and a B-1B Lancer over the Sierra Nevada of Southern California. (Boeing)

reasons, although in reality the development of LO as a black programme prevented the real reason being disclosed. Senior USAF personnel who were privy to LO characteristics quickly realised that such a project would be extremely costly, as the application of the new technology in both design and production would be required on a grand scale.

The radar evading bomber began as a 'black' programme in 1978, initially as Project *Senior C J*. (Note the link between the initials in the project name, and the initials of Clarence Johnson, who was known as 'Kelly' Johnson, head of Lockheed's ADP 'Skunk Works'.) The project was soon renamed as the Advanced Technology Bomber (ATB), with work already under way to study methods of incorporating all possible low observability technology into an intercontinental range bomber. Both Lockheed and Northrop were contenders for the

contract.

Despite the programme being 'black', its existence was reported in a 1980 edition of *Aviation Week and Space Technology*, and was confirmed by the Defense Secretary Harold S Brown a few days later. However, no further mention was made until 1988 when it was revealed that the entire programme had been conducted under the tightest security since the *Manhattan* Project to build the atomic bomb. Several aerospace companies formed consortiums to spread the massive development costs and to generate the necessary technological development base to formulate the finished product. Eventually it was a straight choice between Northrop/Boeing and Lockheed/Rockwell, with the former being selected to construct what appeared to be a very lucrative product, as the Air Force indicated production would be 132 of the new bombers. It was later reported that

Kelly Johnson, who had retired as head of Lockheed's ADP, but retained an interest in the firm's activities, advised Ben Rich, the Skunk Works boss at the time, not to bid too enthusiastically for the contract as the bomber would almost certainly experience cost over-runs and other problems which would cut deeply into any projected profit margins. As events have transpired, Kelly was proved right, as the whole project became the most costly in the history of the Department of Defense and the subject of bitter criticism within political circles!

Northrop was the prime contractor with Boeing, General Dynamics and Vought forming the team to produce the new aircraft, which was given the designation B-2. Not surprisingly Northrop drew heavily on the experience gained with its original flying wing project from four decades earlier. Whereas the F-117 was a multi-faceted design involving flat surfaces at various angles designed to bounce radar signals in different directions, the B-2 was a unique blended wing arrangement. The design team used three-dimensional computer-aided drawings to create the most effective pattern which would give the smallest radar cross section possible. In excess of 100,000 radar cross section images of various flying wing designs were analysed to ascertain the most effective. Each component was fabricated and collectively exposed to more than a half million wind tunnel test hours. Much of the work was carried out at the Northrop Radar Cross Section facility at Tejon Canyon near Palmdale, California.

However, designing the aircraft was only one aspect. Construction was yet another major undertaking,

Far Right: The prototype B-2A (AV1) 82-1066, was revealed to the world outside its Palmdale assembly building in November 1988. The American star was made up of five planviews of the stealth bomber.
Right: The B-2A production line at Palmdale where components built by Northrop, Boeing and Vought were assembled. (Photos Northrop Grumman)

with several manufacturing techniques developed specifically for the programme. Amongst these was the use of ultrasonic cutting equipment, automated tooling using three-dimensional computer-aided systems, as well as laser technology for a number of processes. Every external component had to be designed from scratch with new methods of cutting and assembly. Northrop built the forward section and cockpit area, while Boeing constructed the aft centre and outboard sections. The mid section, as well as all aluminium, titanium and composite parts, was produced by Vought. With several manufacturers producing limited parts of the aircraft, it was simpler for Northrop to maintain secrecy.

The single-most important aspect of the design was the rear of the wing which was shaped into a unique pair of giant 'W's. Powerplants selected were four General Electric F118-GE-110 turbofans which produced 19,000lb (84.52kN) of thrust each. These

were buried deep in the wing, with the exhaust channelled through V-shaped outlets set some distance from the trailing edge to hide the heat source from the ground. To prevent contrails forming at altitude, chioro-flourosulphonic acid is injected into the exhaust. The Hughes AN/APQ-181 low-probability of intercept navigation radar, operating in J-band, is positioned behind specially designed stealthy dielectric panels to enable it to operate normally with the minimum risk of detection. However, during an attack profile, the radar would only be activated sufficiently long enough for the crew to verify their target. The defensive capabilities of the B-2 encompass an electronic warfare (EW) system consisting of the IBM Federal Systems AN/APR-50 radar warning receiver, together with a highly secret defensive aids system.

As stated earlier, the first B-2A, serial 82-1066 — known by the manufacturer as Air Vehicle One (AV1) — emerged into the public

spotlight in November 1988. After ground handling trials and fast runs, the aircraft performed its maiden flight from Palmdale on July 17, 1990. After some rudimentary evaluation of its flight characteristics, the B-2 landed at Edwards AFB to commence the long test programme. The test fleet was increased with the delivery of 82-1067 (AV2) to Edwards AFB on October 19, 1990. Initial handling and airworthiness assessment was completed within 67 flight hours, which included the first aerial refuelling from a KC-10A Extender.

Evaluation of the LO characteristics commenced in October 1990, with some flights being delayed while modifications to the stealth capability were incorporated into AV1. AV2 was engaged on performance trials as ▶

Right: B-2A 88-0329 Spirit of Missouri, seen at the 1995 Paris Air Show, was the first to be delivered to the 509th Bomb Wing at Whiteman AFB, Missouri.

Above: B-2A 89-0127 Spirit of Kansas 'arrives' at RAF Fairford during RIAT '97 having flown non-stop from Whiteman AFB. (Photos AFM - Duncan Cubitt)

Right: The 'billion dollar bomber', which seems to change its shape when seen from different angles, first flew on July 17, 1989.

well as evaluation of load testing. AV3 82-1068 joined the programme in June 1991, the first with a fully operational AN/APQ-181 radar installed. AV3 also had the full avionics mission kit fitted. AV4 82-1069 became the fourth test vehicle in April 1992, and was primarily concerned with the delivery of munitions; the first weapons drop being made by this aircraft on September 4, 1992 involving an inert Mk 84 2,000lb (908kg) bomb. The fifth B-2A serial 82-1070 (AV5) arrived at Edwards AFB in October 1992 for climatic tests as well as evaluation of weapons delivery in conjunction with its LO features. The final test aircraft was 82-1071 (AV6) which was delivered in February 1993.

Even before the test programme had reached the half-way stage, the B-2 began to show deficiencies in its stealth capability. To rectify these the manufacturer incorporated modifications to sections of the leading edge and flying surfaces to reduce the signature within a certain range of frequencies. Furthermore there were problems with the performance of the B-2 within certain parameters. Collectively these did little to assist the programme particularly when requests for funding were being made, with many senior political figures in Washington trying to 'kill off' the stealth bomber. Some questioned the need for such an expensive weapon in view of the reduced threat from Russia and the elimination of the Warsaw Pact. The Air Force had originally identified a requirement for 132 ATBs, although spiralling development costs coupled with the Russian decision to abandon competition in strategic weapons, enabled the Department of Defense to reassess the programme. This was subsequently reduced to 75, and later to just 20 plus the prototype; the latter being the minimum number required to fulfil the radically changed SIOP (Single Integrated Operations Plan). The role of the B-2 was changed significantly from that of nuclear weapons delivery, to encompass conventional and SMART munitions.

The B-2 was still a 'black' programme when the first five production aircraft were ordered in 1988. Additional orders were placed in 1989 for three aircraft and in 1990 for a further two before Congress froze acquisition at 16. The decision left the USAF with the potential problem that it would be unable to provide an effective operational capability with less than 20 aircraft. Congress was eventually persuaded to release the funds for the remainder to be ordered with one more in 1992, and the final four from the fiscal year 1993 budget. However, the money was only to be made available on the proviso that problems with the LO be rectified before delivery of production aircraft to Air Combat Command (AAC). At that time the unit cost per aircraft, including 'black' money allocated for the development programme, had reached a staggering $2,220 million — truly the 'billion dollar bomber'.

Fifteen years after the ATB programme was launched, the first delivery to an operational unit took place, with the 509th Bomb Wing at Whiteman AFB, Missouri, receiving 88-0329 Spirit of Missouri on December 17, 1993. Prior to the arrival, Whiteman AFB had been upgraded with the construction of

'truly the billion dollar bomber'

giant aircraft barns to house individual B-2As. Further deliveries have consisted of four aircraft during 1994 (88-0328 *Spirit of Texas* delivered August 31; 88-0330 *Spirit of California* d/d August 7; 88-0331 *Spirit of South Carolina* d/d December 30; 88-0332 *Spirit of Washington* d/d October 30), three in 1995 (89-0127 *Spirit of Kansas* d/d February 17; 89-0128 *Spirit of Nebraska* d/d June 28; 89-0129 *Spirit of Georgia* d/d November 14), five in 1996 (90-0040 *Spirit of Alaska* d/d January 24; 90-0041 *Spirit of Hawaii* d/d January 11; 92-0700 *Spirit of Oklahoma* d/d July 3; 93-1085 *Spirit of Florida* d/d May 15; 93-1086 *Spirit of Kitty Hawk* d/d August 30) and two in 1997 (93-1087 *Spirit of Pennsylvania* in October; plus the refurbished and upgraded second B-2A 82-1067 *Spirit of Ohio*. Another B-2, 93-1088 *Spirit of Louisiana* was delivered on November 10, 1997. The remaining six development and test aircraft will also be brought up to full production standard.

The batch of six development B-2As was to be constructed to interim standard to perform all the necessary test duties, although it soon became apparent to Northrop that a series of Block numbers would have to be allocated to determine the various categories of operational capability. Aircraft production was divided into three Blocks, commencing with Block 10 which consisted of the second B-2A to number 16 (AV-2 to AV-16), capable of carrying B83 nuclear bombs or 16 Mk 84 2,000lb conventional bombs. Three aircraft were to be constructed to Block 20

Left: The distinctive 'flying wing' shape of the Spirit was foreshadowed by Northrop's bombers of the 1940s, the XB-35 and YB-49. (Photos Northrop-Grumman)

configuration, identified as airframes AV-17 to AV-19, with the final two AV-20 and AV-21 being to Block 30 standard. Block 20 involved the fitment during manufacture of a global positioning aided targeting system coupled with a GPS aided munitions guidance capability to enable the B-2 to have an interim, near precision strike capacity earlier than originally planned.

The version is capable of carrying 16 of these GPS guided weapons and could also house the B61 nuclear bomb. The final version is Block 30 which has the full precision guided munitions capability

including provision for 16 JDAMs housed on a rotary launcher in the bomb bay. Other types of munitions which will be compatible are Mk 82 500lb bombs, as well as cluster bombs such as the sensor fused weapon, the M117 750lb bomb, and Mk 62 aerial mines. Block 30 also incorporates fully operational defensive and offensive avionics, a sophisticated mission planning system and additional operating modes compatible with the synthetic aperture radar. The capabilities of the B-2 were overtaken by events as the sudden end of the *Cold War* forced planners to reassess the most suitable

Below: B-2A 89-0128 Spirit of Nebraska *on static display at Nellis showing off its unstealthy but heavy-duty undercarriage.* (AFM - Steve Fletcher

Above: The unmistakable shape of a 'Spirit in the Sky' crosses the threshold of Whiteman AFB's runway.

operational mode with the light of the new détente. Instead of performing high-level nuclear weapons delivery as the primary mission, the B-2 added that of low and medium level operations with SMART conventional munitions.

However, changes were made during production from the eleventh example, which was delivered in July 1996 and became the first of the Block 20 machines capable of delivering precision munitions. All aircraft from 90-0040 (AV-16) had the latest weapons fit incorporated during manufacture. Subsequently

B-2A 88-0329 (AV-9) was upgraded to Block 30 standard and was returned to Whiteman AFB during late 1997. Plans are in place for all of the remainder to be cycled through Northrop at Palmdale for upgrade to Block 30 configuration.

The Pentagon announced in March 1996 that the President had authorised funding to enable the prototype B-2 flight test airframe 82-1066 (AV-1) to be upgraded to full operational standard using $493 million which Congress added to the FY1996 defence budget for the stealth bomber programme. The

upgrade will increase the B-2 inventory to 21 operational aircraft and will see the production line kept open until July 2000.

Funding had previously been made available for another test aircraft, 82-1067 (AV-2), to be upgraded, with this example having been the first of the six test airframes to enter operational service when it was flown to Whiteman AFB during the summer of 1997. AV-1 was constructed with less capable low observability characteristics, which will be upgraded to the same capabilities as those from Block 30 production.

During its test phase, AV-1 was used to evaluate the flying qualities of the design, and to verify the low observability of Block 10 production before the airframe was placed in external storage with Northrop at Palmdale.

The cost of the entire B-2 programme was such that had it not been 'black' for almost a decade, many in Congress who have their hand on the tiller of the defence budget would almost certainly have called for a halt before the first aircraft was even built.

The classification of 'black' works as a double-edged sword enabling an innovative project to proceed while at the same time hiding the true cost until it is too late to be abandoned.

Right: A total of 16 Northrop B-2A Spirits had been delivered to the 393rd Bomb Squadron of the 509th Bomb Wing at Whiteman AFB by the end of 1997. (Photos - Northrop Grumman)

THE PHANTOM WORKS:

THE PHANTOM WORKS was not simply McDonnell Aircraft's version of Lockheed's Skunk Works. While the Phantom Works shares the basic initial focus of the Skunk Works brief on classified programmes, it has since gone in different directions.

Its origins were in McDonnell Aircraft's New Aircraft and Missile Products, and Advanced Systems Technologies Divisions. These predecessors handled classified programmes, along with those from the 'white' world, from the 1960s to the 1990s. The Phantom Works mission has also changed with the current decrease in US defence spending and with McDonnell Douglas' recent acquisition by Boeing.

The name was chosen in conscious imitation of its Lockheed predecessor, but also to invoke the way that McDonnell Aircraft designed its most famous product, the F-4 Phantom II, which was done by a small team in a short time. The Phantom Works has adopted the 'Phantom II' cartoon character long associated with that aircraft as its unofficial logo.

The Phantom Works has been, since August 1997, the research and advanced development unit of Boeing's Information, Space, and Defense Systems (ISDS) organisation which adds, to the St Louis-based McDonnell Aircraft ('MacAir'), Boeing's Space Systems and Information and Communications Systems divisions. Because of its name recognition and to show its McDonnell origins, Boeing has kept the name.

The Works differs from its predecessors in other firms. The original Lockheed Skunk Works was an independent operation, small and centrally located, and kept separate from the rest of the Lockheed organisation for security reasons. Today the Phantom Works has gone in different directions. It has 4,500 employees working in facilities in 12 states. Rather than erecting 'Chinese walls', it draws on personnel from throughout Boeing ISDS. These are largely organised in teams of one to 200 people, averaging about 25, to support both external customers, largely in the Department of Defense, as well as internal customers within the vast Boeing ISDS organisation. These teams are intended to provide a task-specific focus on customer needs. The management structure is intended to allow a team with detailed knowledge of the customer's requirements to call upon the vast resources of Boeing ISDS to meet them. The work with external customers has resulted in about $600 million in sales.

Unlike the Skunk Works, the Phantom Works is focused, in the words of its Executive Vice President, Donald Swain, "Primarily on improving the bottom and top lines of the ISDS business units".

While aircraft have been its most visible products, it has also worked on improving manufacturing and R&D processes, designing and improving weapons and munitions; launch vehicles and space systems, and C⁴I (command, control, communications, computers and intelligence) technologies. The Phantom Advanced Systems Groups include Advanced Weapons, Advanced Rotorcraft, Advanced Transport, Advanced Space, Advanced C⁴I and Open Architecture

Like the Skunk Works, McDonnell Douglas's Phantom Works has gone from the 'black' of the 1960s to the 'white' of the 1990s. A report by David C Isby.

Above: *The Waterloo of the 'black' world was the McDonnell Douglas/General Dynamics A-12 Advanced Tactical Aircraft (ATA), the mock-up of which is seen here in the Phantom Works.*

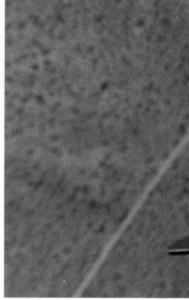

Avionics.

The Phantom Works will handle only the initial conceptualisation and design and the research, development, testing and evaluation (RDT&E) phase of new systems and weapons. Any engineering and manufacturing development (EMD) or production would be dealt with elsewhere in ISDS. But the two-ship X-36 programme showed how the Phantom Works can, when dealing with a specialised R&D programme, bring it all to fruition.

The age of 'black'

McDonnell Douglas was a player when the golden age of the 'black' world opened in the 1970s. The appeal of making aircraft programmes 'black' was readily apparent for both policy and technological reasons. Most classified aircraft programmes started out as relatively inexpensive research and development (R&D) programmes which meant that they were affordable at a time when the post-Vietnam cuts led to the 'hollow forces' era. They also provided a justification for some of those cuts:

if there was something better being developed in secret, decision-makers could justify cutting more advanced 'white' programmes, as President Jimmy Carter did to the B-1A bomber programme after learning of the 'black' development of the B-2 bomber and stealth cruise missiles.

Post-Vietnam distrust of the military by the Congress and the Press (which was certainly reciprocated) meant that many thought that only classified programmes could survive hostile scrutiny. But there were also valid technological reasons for the rise of the 'black' world. The US entered the microchip revolution before its Soviet competitors. Keeping programmes classified denied the Soviets not only knowledge needed for countermeasures, but that of where to invest their own R&D resources. Even where the Soviets thoroughly understood the underlying science, 'black' programmes kept them from realising that it had been weaponised.

McDonnell Douglas' most famous 'black' programme while teamed

with General Dynamics — was also the Waterloo of the 'black' world: the A-12 Advanced Tactical Aircraft (ATA). Nicknamed the 'Dorito', from its resemblance to the triangular corn chip, this stealthy attack aircraft was to replace the US Navy's A-6s and the USAF's F-111s. Pushed by the Navy during the first Reagan term, high levels of classification and strict compart-mentalisation contributed to the familiar woes of any new combat aircraft design trying to use untried technologies. Costs increased and the first flights and in-service dates receded. Finally, in 1991, with US defence spending cuts increasing, the A-12 was cancelled. The programme dissolved into lengthy litigation, still in progress — which ended up revealing that inconsistent government management decisions were the main reason for the cost rises and delays. In the end, the success belonged not to the engineers or the pilots, but the lawyers.

X-36

Today, with most of its work 'white' or even unclassified, the Phantom Works aims to apply the focus and speed of 'black' world work to a much larger set of problems. The most visible recent demonstration of the Phantom Works' capabilities and approach is the X-36.

The X-36 was developed by McDonnell Douglas (now succeeded by Boeing) with NASA (costs being split) — NASA being responsible for continued development of the critical technologies being demonstrated. The X-36 is a tail-less, quarter-scale remotely-piloted

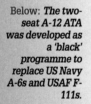

Left: *The design, production and flight testing of two subscale X-36 research vehicles costs only $17 million.*

vehicle (RPV) intended to demonstrate the use of innovative thrust-vectoring exhaust nozzles and split-aileron control technologies. These have the potential to make future combat aircraft incredibly manoeuvrable while reducing weight, drag and radar cross section. The ailerons are able to raise and lower asymmetrically to provide roll control.

The X-36 had its origins in a 1993 proposal by McDonnell Douglas to build a demonstrator for technologies to enhance tail-less agile flight developed in wind tunnels since 1989. With NASA and McDonnell Douglas agreeing to cost sharing in 1994, the Phantom Works designed, developed and produced the prototype X-36 in just 28 months. The total programme cost, including design and production of two flyable X-36s and the flight testing programme itself, is only $17 million.

By using an RPV to demonstrate these technologies, the X-36 was made twice as fast and ten times cheaper than a full-size piloted aircraft. The Phantom Works was able to achieve this combination of low cost and rapid realisation by using a range of advanced, low-cost, design and manufacturing technologies that have been developed in-house. Rapid avionics prototyping through the use of advanced software development tools, the use of low-cost tooling moulds; curing composite skins at low temperatures without the use of autoclaves and high speed machining of unitised assemblies were among its developed capabilities that made the X-36

programme possible.

The McDonnell Douglas (now Boeing) X-36 stands in a long line of US experimental aircraft dating back to the Bell X-1 of 1947 but it resembles nothing so much as the ultimate model airplane. Its loaded weight is but 1,300lb (590kg), with an 11ft (3.3m) wingspan and 19ft (5.8m) long. Its Williams Research F112 turbojet provides about 700lb (317kg) of thrust. A pilot in a ground-based 'virtual cockpit', including a head-up display (HUD), remotely flies the X-36 through an off-the-shelf digital fly-by-wire system, with a video camera in the nose providing visibility.

The X-36 arrived at NASA's Dryden Flight Research Center at Edwards AFB, California, in 1996 for a 25-flight test programme,

demonstrating the potential advantages of its high manoeuvrability technology. The three-stage test programme, concluded in November, 1997, was considered highly successful.

Hypersonic flight

McDonnell Aircraft's research into re-entry heating when designing the original Mercury space capsules was the origin of its expertise in dealing with extremes of heat; this has led to involvement in the field of nuclear fusion research, providing shielding. It has also led to its expertise in the area of hypersonic flight in the atmosphere. With the revival of interest in hypersonic flight the earlier National Aerospace Plane (NASP) was cancelled in 1993 — for both aircraft

Left: *Advanced rotorcraft, such as the McDonnell Douglas Canard Rotor/Wing concept, are developed at the Phantom Works. (Photos McDonnell Douglas)*

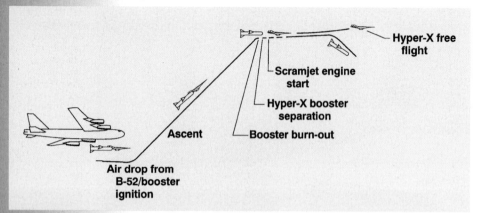

Hyper-X free flight

Scramjet engine start

Hyper-X booster separation

Ascent

Booster burn-out

Air drop from B-52/booster ignition

Above: Another joint project between the Phantom Works and NASA is the design of the scramjet-powered Mach 7 Hyper-X test vehicle scheduled for flight testing next year. (McDonnell Douglas)

Below: The latest product of the Phantom Works is the X-36 tail-less unmanned research aircraft, a joint project with NASA to develop a prototype fighter aircraft designed for stealth and agility.

and cruise missiles, the Phantom Works has been a major participant in advancing this technology. Indeed, in 1997, a study said that a scramjet-powered B-1B size Mach 10 aircraft, with a 5,280 mile (8,500km) radius of action and a 11,000lb (5,000kg) payload, was feasible.

The Phantom Works has designed Hyper-X, a NASA programme to test scramjet propulsion technology at speeds of Mach 5 to Mach 10. The Hyper-X test vehicle, intended to be boosted to altitude on a Pegasus launch vehicle carried under the wing of NASA's NB-52, uses the same basic design as a potential Mach 10 aircraft. While a NcDonnell Douglas design, four flight vehicles with a 5ft (1.5m) wingspan and 12ft (3.6m) long — are being built by Micro Craft of Tullahoma, Tennessee. First flight is planned for mid-1999.

Again, affordability was a prime objective. The NASP (see page ??) cost billions and never flew. Each of the four Hyper-X flight vehicles is to fly once and the entire programme is to cost only $170 million, (the four flight vehicles accounting for $33.4 million). If the Hyper-X reaches its design goal of Mach 7 flight, it will be the fastest-ever air-breathing winged aircraft.

Technology development

Developing new technologies and processes are part of the Phantom Works' mission. One of the most significant achievements was its development of automatic fibre placement capabilities for use with composite material structural components. This has allowed complex shapes to be fabricated with uniform high quality and no waste of expensive composite materials in the manufacture of large, complex composite parts, such as the C-17's landing gear pod fairings. Improvement in using structural composites was also the goal of new metal arc sprayed composite tooling for the AV-8B's forward fuselage side panels. This substantially reduced the cost and lead time of autoclave tools.

The Phantom Works has developed high-speed machining techniques that have been used in the production of the F/A-18E/F Hornet for the US Navy. This aircraft is 25% larger than its predecessor, the F/A-18C/D, but has 42% fewer structural parts as a result of these improvements. In addition to reducing the number of parts, this has also reduced the number of fasteners and assembly tools required which, in turn, reduce assembly time and labour hours, saving money. These new machining technologies apply to aluminum as well as composites, literally sculpting sections of the aircraft out of aluminum using highly precise Ingersoll computer-guided machine tools.

Other advances have been in the areas of modelling and simulation,

flexible tooling and high-speed machinery. Consistent with the emphasis on the bottom line, the current goals have been to achieve savings in affordability and reducing the time to make innovations available to customers. Many of these advances will migrate into Boeing's conventional aircraft business, where automated fastening techniques are seen as a key area where they are behind its arch-rival Airbus, which has accurately automated almost the entire process of riveting and joining together sections of aircraft.

Aircraft upgrades

During the Falklands War, one Royal Navy Sea Harrier pilot on final approach to a carrier in fog claimed he did not know he had landed until he heard the deck crew applauding. The Phantom Works, in a two-month programme in 1996, provided this pilot's US Marine Corps counterparts with a more reliable blind landing aid for vertical approaches to carriers. The Self-Contained Approach (SCA) software was demonstrated only two months after the programme began, combining the Phantom Works' rapid prototyping capability and commercial off the shelf (COTS) software to allow the AV-8B Harrier's existing on-board navigation systems to precisely calculate position and velocity relative to a ship's deck or other small landing area. SCA testing was continued in 1997.

The Phantom Works Common Operational Flight Program (COFP) also aims to improve the software that today is vital to any state-of-the-art combat aircraft by improving the reusability of software and increasing its ability to run on COTS computers. This software, flight tested starting in 1996 on F/A-18Cs and AV-8Bs, has applicability to future design programmes, such as that of the Joint Strike Fighter. The use of reusable software could cut the cost of software design and maintenance by as much as half, while the ability to use commercial processors will also increase affordability.

The High Stability Engine Control Program saw the Phantom Works joining with NASA, the USAF, and Pratt & Whitney to develop and test an advanced engine control system that will potentially prevent compressor stalls and engine failures by using a high-speed computerised sensor and appropriate software to respond to high levels of engine inlet airflow

turbulence or distortion, which could increase the manoeuvrability of future fighter planes. In 1997, the system went through a two-stage flight test programme on a modified F-15 that was able to use this upgrade throughout a wide flight envelope.

Weapons programmes

The Phantom Works recently focused on two air-delivered munitions programmes. It is developing prototypes and testing the JDAM (Joint Direct Attack Munition) and the JASSM (Joint Air-to-Surface Stand-off Missile). McDonnell Douglas won the competition for the bomb portion and integration of the JDAM in October, 1995 and it has already entered low-rate initial production. The Phantom Works has been a key player in McDonnell Douglas' entry in the JASSM programme with a low-cost, low-risk design that is in direct competition with a formerly classified design from Lockheed's Skunk Works. The competition winner is currently scheduled to be selected in July 1998.

Another programme has been McDonnell Douglas' concept for a Small Smart Bomb. This is a stealthy 250lb (113kg) weapon intended for internal carriage by F-22s and other low-observable aircraft. Although it would only have some 50lb (22kg) of explosive — a high-technology composition that meets new requirements for insensitive munitions — the objective is for its high accuracy to give it a hard target destruction capability now only equalled by larger bombs. It will be capable of penetrating 6ft (1.8m) of concrete. Its accuracy against such point targets will be provided by multiple guidance technologies, including an INS, jam-proof GPS, and LIDAR.

Left & Below: *Two advanced weapons prototypes, the Joint Direct Attack Munitions (JDAM) and the Joint Air-to-Surface Stand-off Missile (JASSM) were designed and built at the Phantom Works. (McDonnell Douglas/Steve Fletcher)*

The future of the 'black' world

The current direction of the Phantom Works shows how it has adapted to the end of the *Cold War*. The heyday of classified aircraft programmes is over, in part because of changing times, decreasing defence spending and numbers of new aircraft, but also because of some of the more spectacular failures in the 'black' world.

The A-12 programme was the graveyard not only of many careers, but also, reportedly, of many even more classified programmes that were sheltering under it. Because of this, the book-keeping of this doomed programme, a decade later, is still not straight. The B-2, in its long 'black' gestation, was unable to build up constituencies for its deployment in the country, the Congress, or even in the US Air Force. This contributed to B-2 production being limited to 21 and being considered at the bottom of the USAF's priority list.

As of 1998, there is at least one and possibly more unannounced types of 'black' aircraft flying, the USAF equivalents of the Loch Ness Monster, with each unconfirmed sighting being eagerly interpreted. Mac Air may have had a part in such aircraft. But future programmes of

this type are more likely to involved UAVs (unmanned aerial vehicles - see page ?) or classified upgrades to existing aircraft. 'Black' weapons, sensors, or communications capabilities that would surprise a future enemy are all likely to be more numerous than aircraft types. It is likely that, given the Phantom Works' range of capabilities, a number of these have started there.

So, with the great days of the 'black' programmes passing, the Phantom Works is now working in the cold light of day, successfully applying the management styles that thrived in the 'black' world — intense focus, high accountability and empowerment of a small team, thorough knowledge of what the people paying for the programme actually need with the goal being not a handful of secret aeroplanes, but an improved bottom line.

Left: *The Hyper-X test vehicle could be used to develop a Mach 10 unmanned reconnaissance aerial vehicle (URAV) or even an unmanned combat aerial vehicle (UCAV). (Pete West)*

Recce To

Right: *U-2R 80-1096 of the 9th RW/99th RS from Beale AFB seen over the Sierra Nevada carrying mission equipment super-pods and a GPS on the trailing edge of the port wing. (Ted Carlson)*

Below: *A U-2R climbs away from Beale towards the nearby Sierra Nevada carrying two mission equipment superpods. (Lockheed-Martin)*

LOCATED 40 MILES (64km) north of Sacramento, California's capital, and close to the Nevada State border, Camp Beale opened in 1942 as a training site for US Army armoured and infantry divisions. During World War Two, the camp's 86,000 acres were home to more than 60,000 soldiers, a prisoner-of-war camp and a 1,000 bed hospital.

In 1948 the camp was transferred to the US Air Force which conducted bombardier and navigation training until 1951 when the Beale Bombing and Gunnery Range was activated.

In May 1959, the base came under the command of Strategic Air Command (SAC) and the 4126th Strategic Wing was activated, equipped with the new KC-135 Stratotankers. On January 18, 1960, the 31st Bombardment Squadron (BS) with B-52s arrived at Beale to become part of the Wing. The 14th Air Division moved to Beale from Travis AFB a week later and the 4126th was redesignated the 456th Strategic Aerospace Wing in 1963.

On October 15, 1964, the Department of Defense announced that Beale AFB would be the home of the new, supersonic reconnaissance aircraft, the SR-71 Blackbird and the 4200th Strategic

o w n u s a

David Oliver visits Beale Air Force Base, California, former home of the USAF's Blackbirds and for the past 17 years, the U-2 Dragon Lady.

Reconnaissance Wing (SRW) was subsequently activated on January 1, 1965. The new wing received its first aircraft, a T-38 Talon advanced trainer, in July 1965 while the first SR-71, assigned to the 99th SRS, arrived at Beale on January 7, 1966.

Later that year, the 9th SRW, that began as the 9th Observation Group in 1922, and its 1st Strategic Reconnaissance Squadron — the history of which dated back to the 1st Aero Squadron in 1913 — replaced the 4200th SRW.

Build-up, development, research, the training of combat crews and perfecting intelligence systems and techniques was to be the 9th SRW's mission, and it remains so today.

Apart from the SR-71's operational roles (see *Senior Crown* - page 21) the Wing's aircrews achieved a series of spectacular record-breaking flights with the Blackbird. In 1971, Lt Cols Thomas B Estes and Dewain C Vick flew 15,000 miles (24,140km) in 10½ hours, while Majs James V Sullivan and his Reconnaissance Systems Officer (RSO) Noel F Widdifield, broke the transatlantic record between New York and London with a flight time of 1 hour 56 minutes! The same aircraft, flown on the return flight by Capt Harold B Adams and RSO Maj William C Machorak, established yet

Above: Groundcrew working on U-2S 80-1085 on the ramp in front of the Beale AFB control tower. Note the sun shade over the cockpit and the open E-bay door beneath the engine intake. Left: A U-2R lines up for take-off from Beale AFB's runway. Note the wing-mounted outrigger which falls away on take-off. (AFM-Duncan Cubitt)

another record by flying from London to Los Angeles in 3 hours 47 minutes.

Headlines were made again in July 1976, when the SR-71 shattered six speed and altitude world records previously held by the Blackbird's predecessor, the YF-12A and Soviet MiG-25s.

That same year, the USAF announced a consolidation of its reconnaissance activities which included the merger of the U-2 aircraft from the 100th SRW at Davis-Monthan AFB with Beale's aircraft. In August 1981, the 9th SRW's 99th SRS accepted the USAF's first TR-1 *Dragon Lady* aircraft, a development of the U-2, and the 4029th Strategic Reconnaissance Training Squadron (SRTS) was activated, with responsibility for training all U-2/TR-1 pilots. This unit took over training SR-71 pilots two years later and in July 1986, it was redesignated the 5th SRTS.

The 100th Air Refuelling Wing, flying specially modified KC-135Q

tanker aircraft to refuel the SR-71, was transferred from March AFB to Beale in March 1983.

US budget restrictions forced the retirement of USAF SR-71s on January 26, 1990, and its parent unit, the 1st Reconnaissance Squadron replaced the 5th SRTS at Beale. Following a post-Gulf War reorganisation in September 1991, the 9th SRW became the 9th Wing and two years later, the 9th Reconnaissance Wing (RW).

However, after much debate about the Blackbird's 'premature' retirement, Congress directed the re-activation of three SR-71s in 1994, and their return to operational status by September 1, 1995.

These were assigned to the 9th RW's Detachment 2 at Edwards AFB, California, but before they were declared operational in September 1997, funding for the Blackbirds was again withdrawn —

this time by President Clinton — and the three aircraft were again assigned to 'inviolate' storage at Edwards a month later.

The only flying unit resident at Beale AFB remains the 9th RW, although it is about to be joined by an AFRC Air Refuelling Wing (ARW), the 940th ARW, whose KC-135E Stratotankers are in the process of moving from nearby McClellan AFB to Beale.

The 9th RW currently includes: the 1st RS, the 99th RS, the 9th Intelligence Squadron, the 9th Operations Support Squadron and the 5th RS located at Osan Air Base, South Korea. Other units comprise: Detachment 1 at RAF Akrotiri, Cyprus; Operating Location-France (OL-Fr) at Istres; and the 4402nd RS (Provisional) at Al Kharj, Saudi Arabia. The 1st RS recruits and trains all the USAF U-2 pilots, all of whom are volunteers with a minimum of 1,500 flying hours, from diverse backgrounds. These include a number from Air Transport and Training Commands as well as those from the fast-jet

community. Before undertaking three evaluation flights in a two-seat U-2 trainer, they are all given a thorough medical and physiological screening, as the high-altitude long-endurance U-2 flights put different requirements on a pilot to any other form of combat flying. As the U-2 handles much like an over-powered glider and is notoriously difficult to land, many pilots with heavy aircraft experience, such as the C-130 and B-52, prove to be more adept as U-2 pilots than some 'fighter' jocks — one of whom recently gave up after only two of his allotted three evaluation flights. On average, some 20 pilots a year will be accepted for evaluation, 35-40% of this total will fail to be selected.

Those who are selected are assigned to the 1st RS which currently has 19 instructor pilots, for operational training. The initial phase of six dual flights — five instructional and one evaluation — take place in the Squadron's four two-seat U-2RT/STs, and is followed by a solo flight in a U-2R, formerly designated TR-1. The pilot then continues to the high-altitude mission qualification during which all sorties, except three, are flown solo. Every year, two or three former U-2 pilots who have completed a ground tour, will return to the 1st RS for requalification which consists of some nine flights, most of which are solo. After successfully completing their training courses, U-2 pilots are assigned to the 99th RS.

Having a unique history of operating USAF's high-altitude reconnaissance assets over many of

the world's trouble spots for more than three decades, the 99th Reconnaissance Squadron is very much a front line combat unit. Its latest version of the 44-year-old design, the re-engined and upgraded U-2S, which is still being delivered to the Squadron, is powered by a more powerful and efficient turbojet, the 18,300lb st General Electric F101-GE-F29 turbo fan that gives it improved performance, endurance and payload.

To lessen the pilot's workload, a new autopilot has also been fitted along with some digital controls and a multi-function display. The U-2S is also equipped with the latest suite of 'quick-change' sensors that have been developed following intelligence gathering operations during the Gulf War and Bosnia. These include an integrated E-Systems Commander's Tactical Terminal (CTT), enhanced Advanced Synthetic Aperture Radar System (ASARS-2) sensor with improved moving target indicator (MTI) capability and GPS, plus the SYERS panoramic electro-optical (EO) camera, and the *Senior Ruby* Elint and *Senior Spear* Comint

systems. For pilot continuation and instrument training, the 99th RS uses 12 black-painted two-seat T-38As. On average, U-2 pilots fly 8-10 hours a month in the Talon.

Flying the U-2

Prior to any U-2 mission, pilots start by visiting the 9th Physiological Support Squadron. In fact, two pilots are assigned to any operational mission — one acts as a reserve should the primary pilot fail his pre-mission medical. Located adjacent to the flight line, the 9th PSS is where all the pilots' safety equipment is stored and maintained. This includes the new S-1034 pressurised flying suit — each pilot is assigned two S-1034s at $150,000 each, which he must wear for at least an hour before take-off, breathing 100% pure oxygen — and the ejection-seat life support pack which has remained much the same for the past 20 years. The PSS also operates decompression chambers and a hyperbaric chamber which can be used in emergency treatment for decompression sickness, air embolism, carbon dioxide poisoning

Above: *U-2RT 60-1091 was the last two-seat trainer to be produced, delivered to the 9th SRW in 1998. Note the two-tier sun shades and extended airbrakes. (AFM-Alan Warnes)*

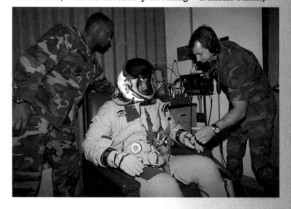

Right: *A Desert Storm veteran, U-2R 80-1081's mission tally with 1704th RS (Provisional) at Taif in Saudi Arabia was 13 Scuds and two patrol boats. (Pete West)*

and gas gangrene. Uniquely for an operational combat aircraft, it is the reserve pilot who carries out the pre-flight inspection of the U-2 on the flight line, highlighting an extremely high degree of trust and confidence in each other's professionalism. The assigned pilot then climbs into a bus carrying a portable life support unit and is driven to his aircraft. There he is assisted up the step ladder and into the confined cockpit to be strapped in and attached to the on-board oxygen system by his crew chief.

Lt Col Bruce *Boogie* Jinneman, a former B-52 pilot, outlines the 9th RW's current role. "We now have more requirements for our services than ever before. Apart from USAF strategic and tactical recce missions, psychological operations (CYOPs) and the nuclear intelligence (NUCINT) role, plus our

operational training, we undertake peacekeeping, humanitarian, search and rescue, environmental and UN support missions in four locations. The 99th RS has 54 assigned pilots and fewer than 20 operational aircraft, others are still being upgraded. On average the pilots fly two or three U-2 'low-level' training missions a month while at Beale — about eight to ten flying hours.

"However, the hours increase during their 60-day overseas deployments to one of the Wing's four detachments. Pilots go on TDY after six months with the 99th RS — two-month deployments followed by two months back at Beale. The 4402nd RS (Provisional) at Al Kharj in Saudi Arabia is back in the headlines following Saddam Hussein's threat to throw out UN weapons inspectors and shoot

down U-2s overflying Iraq. So far the flights have continued at the request of the United Nations — and none have been shot down."

The U-2s are still busy over the Balkans in support of SFOR with Operation *Decisive Endeavour*. The aircraft operating from Det 1 at Akrotiri and OL-Fr at Istres are supported by the 48th Intelligence Squadron via its Deployable Ground Station 2 (DGS-2) which is based at Beale. The DGS-2 maintains direct data links with signal and imagery sensors aboard the U-2s through a forward deployed system known as *Forward Stretch*. Intelligence products are disseminated in near real-time to operational decision-makers in the area of operations such as the SFOR HQ in Bosnia.

Asked if the 1st RS's mission will change in the near future, Lt Col Mario Buda, its commander, answers: "Probably not. It will evolve somewhat. Also some of the equipment will change to make the aircraft easier or safer to fly. Some of the things that are 'hot' right now are an angle-of-attack indicator that will tell the pilot when the aircraft is in an aerodynamic stall. Another item is a single-piece windscreen. The current windscreen has metal frames that block the pilot's view."

With the detachment in Istres due to close this year, the U-2 may be seen again in the UK — the type having been first deployed to England with the 17th Reconnaissance Wing at RAF Alconbury in February 1983, and more recently at RAF Fairford during Operation *Deny Flight*.

From the very early days of its USAF career, several RAF pilots have flown the U-2 on exchange postings and as the RAF's last high-altitude long-endurance reconnaissance aircraft, the venerable Canberra PR.9 is nearing the end of its long career, RAF pilots may again be offered the opportunity of flying the *Dragon Lady* in the future along with those of other NATO countries, few of which have any comparable reconnaissance assets.

Right: *Instrument and continuation training for U-2 pilots of the 9th RW is carried out on T-38A Talons assigned to the 99th RS at Beale.*

Below: *The groundcrew assist the pilot of Dragon Lady 80-1082 to unstrap, following a low-level training mission from Beale. (Photos AFM-Duncan Cubitt)*

COOL, DARK & QUIET

The RAH-66 Comanche Stealth Helicopter — No longer a contradiction in terms. Frank Colucci explains.

ROTORCRAFT ARE CURSED with the same visual, radar, infra-red, acoustic and electronic signatures that betray fixed wing aircraft — only worse. To do their jobs, helicopters press closer to the earth and potential enemies. They are therefore easier to see, hear and electronically detect than faster, higher-flying platforms. Whirling rotor systems generate distinctive Doppler radar returns and unsuppressed engine exhausts forms a cloud attractive to infra-red (IR) homing missiles.

Helicopter signature suppression has long been approached piecemeal and incorporated as an afterthought. However, the Boeing-Sikorsky RAH-66 Comanche is the first 'white world' development programme to truly integrate Low Observable technology into its design and it hints at how stealthy rotorcraft can be.

The US Army teaches that aircraft survivability is a product of tactics, signature suppression and active countermeasures. With air defence threats now smarter, more sensitive and more diverse, all signatures are deadly giveaways. While it may be impossible to make helicopters invisible under all conditions, signature reduction can allow rotorcraft to get closer to their targets without detection. Suppressing signatures also reduces the amount of power and the number of expendables (flare and chaff cartridges) required for active countermeasures. More than any helicopter before, the Comanche relies on reduced detectability and longer-ranged sensors to 'see without being seen' and 'shoot without being shot at.'

X-Rotors

Reports published in 1995 described stealth helicopters tested on the Groom Lake, Nevada, ranges around 1990. One Black programme was supposedly based on the X-Wing publicly unveiled on the Sikorsky S-72 Rotor Systems Research Aircraft (RSRA) in 1986. A conceptual X-wing was expected to take off vertically like a helicopter and stop its rotor in cruising flight with two wings swept forward and two aft. It promised fixed-wing range and speeds to 450kts (833km/h), and it could eliminate the conspicuous Doppler return of a helicopter rotor. Even though the broad-chord composite rotor system

Above: The RAH-66 Comanche is the first helicopter with a truly integrated approach to signature reduction. (Photos Boeing)

Left: Reports of rotary-wing 'black' programmes include an X-wing as shown here in this unclassified artist's concept. The 'White' world X-Wing never flew on the S-72 Rotor Systems Research Aircraft (RSRA). (Sikorsky)

Right: The 'toilet bowl' infra-red (IR) exhaust suppresser was rushed into service in Vietnam and remains on some AH-1 Cobras and UH-1 Hueys today.

was built, the RSRA with X-wing never flew and nothing more has been said of the reported 'Black' version. A smaller single-seat helicopter was also reportedly built by the McDonnell Douglas Helicopter Company (now part of Boeing). The silent TE-K (Test and Evaluation Project K) was described as having four curved main rotor blades and a No Tail Rotor (NOTAR) anti-torque system. In different reports, it was credited with a mast-mounted sight, short stub wings, swing-open weapons bays and an angular, riveted shape.

Prominent rivets are unlikely on an aircraft designed for low Radar Cross Section (RCS), but it is likely that rotary-wing demonstrators of various Low Observable technologies have flown. More concrete are the attempts at signature suppression seen on helicopters in service today.

What you do not see

Black Helicopters have become paranoid mythology in the US, but a subdued paint scheme does address at least one dangerous signature. Optically aimed guns remain major air defence threats. Even IR- and laser-guided missiles such as the Stinger and Javelin rely on optical sights to acquire and track their targets. Reducing the visual signature of helicopters therefore counters or negates two of the three main threat mechanisms on the battlefield.

The frontal aspect of the Comanche in formation with a Longbow Apache makes it obvious a smaller aircraft is harder to spot than a larger one. However, dimensions are dictated more by payload than the desire to hide. Low Observable aircraft have to be big enough to hide weapons and fuel internally. There are

Right: The AH-64D Apache has a mast-mounted radar to stay in terrain mask.

nevertheless ways of making all helicopters harder to see.

Obvious attempts to suppress visual contrast started in Vietnam when bright US 'Stars and Bars' gave way to dull black markings. Flat finishes and low-contrast markings are applied today for both visual and IR protection. They are formulated to absorb visual and infra-red wavelengths and reflect at less noticeable parts of the spectrum.

The choice of a camouflage finish naturally depends on the operating environment. The US Army relies on a non-specular green to hide aircraft flying low over all types of terrain day or night. The US Navy and Marine Corps devised grey tactical schemes to be less noticeable at sea or over the beach. The US Air Force repainted MH-53Js and MH-60Gs from European One green and grey to tan and brown for operations in Southeast Asia. Whatever the choice, visual camouflage should not enhance infra-red signature. Saudi Arabia, for example, initially requested its Apaches be painted tan and brown like Black Hawks and Combat Scouts already in service. The request evaporated when IR vulnerability analysis compared the

desert scheme with US Army dark green.

Bright safety markings at mid-span or tip make rotor systems stand out with the 'barber pole' effect seen on some civil helicopters. US military rotor blades are therefore generally painted black.

After the war in Southeast Asia, the US Army installed flat-plate canopies on modernised AH-1S Cobras and a few OH-58C Kiowas to eliminate the tell-tale glint of curved transparencies. While the US Marines never accepted the drag penalty on their SuperCobras — essentially flat transparencies are now standard on most attack helicopters, including the Apache, Tiger, Rooivalk, Mangusta, Mi-28, Ka-50, OH-1 and Comanche.

The most effective solution to visual signatures is night operations. Image intensifiers (Night Vision Goggles - NVG) and thermal imagers (Forward Looking Infra-Red - FLIR) bring helicopters into the 24-hour battle, and hide them from unaided eyes. Likewise, Nap-of-the-Earth (NoE) flying uses trees and terrain to interrupt the line of sight. Variable-intensity 'slime lights' are formation aids visible only at their lowest settings through NVGs. US Army Apaches now wear slightly reflective unit markings visible through NVGs.

Advanced sensor technology enables helicopters to fly low or at night and stand off at greater ranges. Mast-mounted sights and radars, such as those on the OH-58D Kiowa Warrior and AH-64D Longbow Apache, are meant to keep the helicopter and its rotor system hidden and invisible to air defenders. Second-generation FLIR technology in the Comanche's pilotage and targeting systems sees 40% further in good weather and 50% further in fog and rain, compared to today's Apache Target Acquisition and Designation Sight (TADS). The extended sensor range translates into greater stand-off

Left: The very effective 'black hole' suppressers on the Apache hide hot metal parts and dilute the exhaust plume in cruising or hovering flight.

ranges and a less visible helicopter.

Above NoE flight, the vulnerability of a helicopter to visual, radar, and other detection increases with the time the aircraft is unmasked. US Army studies indicate survivability of a scout/attack helicopter falls off sharply after more than ten seconds out of terrain mask. New technology provides ways to keep attack helicopters in the trees. The Denel Rooivalk, for example, claims a 'snapshot' capability that enables the crew to pop up from mask, record sensor imagery, and drop back down to study the picture in safety. The Assisted Target Detection/Classification (ATD/C) algorithms used by the Comanche find and annotate targets for the crew as the helicopter returns to cover.

Longbow millimetre wave radar on the AH-64D and planned for the RAH-66 affords attack crews even greater stand-off ranges and adverse weather capability. Active radar Hellfire also introduces a true fire-and-forget weapon that finds its target on the darkest night.

No reflection

The radar return of a helicopter fuselage is modulated by a turning rotor system. The accentuated Doppler return is very noticeable to air defence radars. The collective Radar Cross Section (RCS) of a helicopter is reduced by careful design and Radar Absorbent Materials (RAM). RCS reduction was never a factor in the design of the big, square Apache, but the RAH-66 is credited with an RCS just 1/600th that of the AH-64. Reduced radar signature is the primary reason the RAH-66 has retractable landing gear and internally stowed weapons in a fuselage styled for stealth.

The Sikorsky S-75 and Bell D-292

demonstrators built for the Advanced Composite Airframe Program (ACAP) in the mid-1980s provided hints of Low Observable shapes. Unlike the Tiger, Rooivalk and earlier attack helicopters, the Comanche is flared and faired to deny radars a strong return. The same design tricks gave the NH-90/TTH-90 maritime/utility helicopter a diamond-shaped fuselage to optimise RCS. Stealth shaping imposes design trade-offs, and Boeing-Sikorsky engineers abandoned a low RCS V-tail on the early Comanche design for a T-tail with better handling qualities.

Composite materials lend themselves to stealth shaping and reduce the weight of Low Observable fairings. They also provide close assembly tolerances to eliminate steps and gaps which reflect radar energy. Non-metallic laminated composites with their low electrical conductivity are naturally Radar Absorbent Materials (RAM), and they can be filled selectively based on the frequency, power and type of threats expected.

Maintenance-intensive RAM is best applied to 'hotspots' of strong return. OH-58Ds of the 18th Airborne Corps received LO fairings and RAM too late for service in the

Gulf War, but kits remain in storage, and some Kiowa Warriors retain their LO nose and other features. LO kits have been fabricated for other US Army helicopters and the Comanche will be fielded with extra protection to be installed when needed.

The distinctive flicker signature of rotor blades makes helicopters particularly noticeable on ground-based and airborne radars. Rotor hub cuffs on the RAH-66 cover highly reflective control linkages, and a shrouded Fantail is canted to deflect radar return downward from the Comanche anti-torque rotor. Swept main rotor tips pay off in aerodynamic performance and reduced radar and acoustic signatures. Advanced blade designs can also incorporate RAM in their structure and provide alternatives to metal erosion strips on their leading edges.

Fly cold

When a Soviet-made, SA-7 *Grail* or Strella first claimed a US Army *Huey* near Dong Ha, Vietnam, in April 1972, it forever changed the battlefield for helicopters. Like first-generation air-to-air missiles, the shoulder-fired SA-7 with its uncooled infra-red seeker, sought hot metal engine parts. Today's missiles seek the gaseous radiation of engine exhaust plumes. Hot metal remains the dominant part of the helicopter's IR signature, but microprocessors and more sensitive missile seekers demand infra-red suppression across all IR bands.

Effective IR suppression addresses hot metal, plume, solar reflection, airframe friction, and the heat of environmental control systems, transmissions and avionics. While newer missiles may be tuned to exhaust plumes, Third World countries have found the old Strella easy to produce and the hot metal seekers will remain a threat.

The toilet-bowl suppresser or Bell Scoop rushed to Vietnam in 1972 hid

Left: OH-58Ds of the 18th Airborne Corps received Low Observable (LO) kits to cover prominent rotor control linkages and other radar reflectors. (Photos Author)

hot metal and turned the plume upwards to disperse it in rotorwash. It was effective against early threats even in the hover and its slight back pressure imposed only a slight power penalty on the engine. The scoop with its associated inlets and oil cooler shield was still used on *Hueys* in *Desert Storm*. A similar arrangement protects the Eurocopter Gazelle.

Hot-metal-plus-plume suppressers are available for many small- and mid-sized helicopters. The suppresser now on single-engined Cobras is credited with a 99% signature reduction for a 1.5% performance penalty. However, to meet modern suppression standards, powerplant engineers estimate plume radiation must be reduced by an order of magnitude. Hot metal signature has to be cut by two orders of magnitude. That requires a 1,000° F tailpipe be cooled to near-ambient temperature with outside air alone. Exhaust suppressers also have to work in both cruising and hovering flight.

The first GE-Sikorsky suppressers for the UH-60 depended on ram-air and were largely ineffective at less than 70 or 80kts. The Hover Infrared Suppression System (HIRSS), now standard on the Black Hawk and the Black Hole suppressers on the Apache, work in the hover. Similar protection is available for the Eurocopter Cougar and Tiger, and the Westland Lynx. The Russian Mi-24 and Mi-17 acquired suppressers in Afghanistan and the Mi-28 *Havoc* has tested a variety of suppresser arrangements. An IR suppresser is being developed for the modernised, four-bladed AH-1W SuperCobra and UH-1N Twin *Huey*. The engine nacelles of the V-22 Osprey have exhaust suppressers

expected to reduce the lock-on area available to a shoulder-fired IR missile to just 5% that presented by today's CH-46. The big CH-47, CH-53, and EH101 still have no exhaust suppressers, but vulnerability studies are examining the value of IR suppressers on the Improved Chinook Helicopter.

Until the RAH-66 Comanche, IR suppression was something to be bolted behind or beside engines. LO shaping adopted by the Comanche for reduced radar return actually lends itself to the high aspect ratio IR suppression schemes studied by the US Army in the 1970s. Ducting exhaust through long, thin slots, reduces the optical thickness of the flow and decreases the emissivity of the gases by making them thinner. Reshaped fluid dynamics produce a shorter plume of hot gas and ejector lobes

in the slot mix the exhaust with extra air.

The RAH-66 suppression scheme draws ambient air down through two slots on top of the Comanche spine, mixes it with exhaust from the two T800 engines, environmental control system and avionics bays, and pumps it out of 15ft (4.5m) long slots beneath each inverted tail shelf. The arrangement mixes air and hot gas once internally and again as it swirls from the ribbon-type ejector. The resulting signature is dominated by skin emissions. It is so low, the baseline Comanche needs no IR jammer. Provision for a jammer is being included to counter future IR threats.

The more effective engine exhaust suppressers are, the more dangerous secondary IR sources become. Canopy glint attracts both human eyes and IR seekers and flat glass is part of survivable design. Insulating jackets have been tested on the Apache Chain Gun. Reflected solar and background radiation and the contrast of bright colours are giveaways to sensitive IR seekers. Low-IR finishes are therefore formulated to absorb ambient infra-red energy and re-radiate at different wavelengths appeared on US Army helicopters in Vietnam in 1972. The principles still apply and the range of colours has grown.

Do not hear this

Noisy rotors, engines, gearboxes, and air intakes all give helicopters distinct and very detectable acoustic signatures. Sound travels four times as fast as the fastest

Left: *The survivability of the V-22 Osprey benefits from 275kts cruising speeds and an acoustic signature less detectable than that of conventional helicopters. (Bell-Boeing)*

helicopters and it provides ample warning to air defenders. Acoustic anti-helicopter mines seeded along NoE approaches and triggered by specific aircraft signatures are an impending threat.

In cruising airplane mode, the Bell-Boeing V-22 tilt rotor is significantly quieter than a helicopter. Osprey engineers calculate the reduced acoustic signature and higher speed of the V-22 will give an enemy on the ground one-eighth the audible warning time provided by a helicopter. The aircraft is moving faster and the noise of the prop-rotors with nacelles down is projected vertically rather than broadcast along the flight path.

Swept tips on main rotor blades help reduce one source of helicopter noise. However, tail rotors are still major contributors to acoustic signature. The four-bladed tail rotor on the AH-64 Apache has blades offset at 55° and 125° to reduce noise. A similar configuration was developed for the MD500E and MD530 helicopters and adopted for the little AH-6/MH-6.

Noise reduction technology developed for the civil market can be applied to military helicopters, but it comes at a price. The successful NOTAR system first applied to the MD520N was evaluated for the AH-6/MH-6 *Little Birds* of the US Army's 160th Special Operations Aviation Regiment. In principle, the protected anti-torque system with less noise and no tail rotor radar flicker meant a safer, even less detectable helicopter. Unfortunately, NOTAR drew more power than a tail rotor and imposed payload and range penalties unacceptable in unique SOF mission profiles. Significantly, Eurocopter chose not to use a Fenestron on the Tiger attack helicopter.

Until the Comanche, military helicopters never had an acoustic requirement. Classified portions of the RAH-66 specifications spell out how noisy the scout-attack helicopter can be and influenced the overall design. The low tip speed of its shrouded blades makes the Fantail quiet. The production Comanche may also be able to reduce the speed of its tail rotor 10% to provide a 'whisper mode' in stealthy surveillance situations.

Electronic warfare

On the modern battlefield, any electronic emanation is a potential giveaway. Helicopter crews need communications discipline. Navigation and targeting systems cannot broadcast the location of the user. Frequency-hopping radios make transmissions tougher to detect and intercept while inertial navigators and the Global Positioning System provide self-contained navigation solutions. Such systems are being integrated into the helicopters in the US, UK and elsewhere. A broader approach is taken by the US Army's Digital Battlefield initiative. With Improved data modems, digital radios and the associated software, situation reports, sensor imagery, and orders are transmitted and received in brief digital bursts.

High Frequency radio with Automatic Link Establishment software enables helicopters hidden in terrain mask to bounce Non Line Of Sight communications off the ionosphere.

In most aircraft the communications/navigation systems are discrete boxes. The Comanche integrates communications, navigation, and targeting capabilities in a centralised architecture. The RAH-66 watching enemy forces will lock its Target Acquisition Subsystem on a target and receive passive range data from the sensor gimbal offset and GPS navigator. Tough as it is to intercept, the TAS laser need not be used. In a momentary databurst, the precise location of the target will be digitally handed off to other 'shooters' who need never see their target. Even active sensors can be designed for stealth. The Longbow Radar on the AH-64D has low sidelobes and a low probability of interception. The same technology is being repacked in a Low Observable radome for the Comanche.

Active countermeasures can and do protect helicopters, but jammers are beacons as well as shields. Integrated signature reduction is a way to evade the threats instead of duelling with them. ◢

Left: *With its multi-faceted fuselage and tail boom, the S-75 demonstrator for the Advanced Composite Airframe Program revealed elements of LO design. (Author)*

Paul Beaver discovers that 'black' in Britain is a dirty word.

T O READ THE mass media, it is possible to create a vision that all new technologies for military aerospace emanate from the USA. Names like 'Phantom Works' and 'Skunk Works' catch the imagination and many millions of research dollars. Yet in Britain, black is very much beautiful but rarely discussed and certainly never shouted about from the top of a desert mesa as in California.

Britain's aerospace industry has been involved in 'black' programmes for nearly a century, it is just that these programmes are not regarded as such. When researching this article, the 'Man from the Ministry' was very unimpressed with the idea of a feature on 'black' programmes. Certainly no briefings on follow-on Tornado or Eurofighter would be forthcoming — new government openness not withstanding. Even industry is unusually reticent to talk about what goes on at British Aerospace's Warton, GEC-Marconi's Stanmore or Shorts' Castlereagh plants. That is not because there are no programmes. Far from it, the

Below: *The Rapier, a forward swept wing (FSW) agile fighter concept submitted to DERA by the design consultants Avpro Ltd before the Sukhoi S-37 was revealed. (Avpro)*

Above: *The British Army's latest 'black' project — a specially modified 'anti-terrorism surveillance' Skyship 600 airship. (David Oliver)*

programmes which are black are to be kept that way. Why? — because although research and development funding is hard to come by, British industry does not require a fickle Congress to approve another bucket load of dollars for a hypersonic reconnaissance aircraft.

"You could say," said a leading industrialist, "that every programme in this factory started life as 'black'. Radar itself was a 'black programme' when Robert Watson-Watt turned Henry Tizard's 'death-ray' experiments into radio ranging and detection immediately prior to World War Two."

Just last year, the British Army completed one of the most secret programmes in its recent history. The Army Airship Trials Unit at the Army Air Corps Centre, Middle

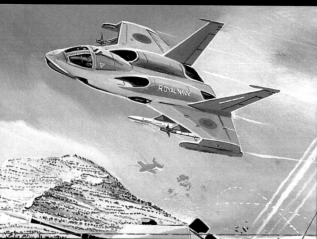

Below: An Avpro Wing-Hulled concept, the Marauder, designed for anti-shipping, search and rescue, special operations and anti-drug smuggling roles. (Avpro)

Right: An alternative to the Royal Navy version of JSF, which may be a contender for the Navy's Future Carrier-borne Aircraft (FCA). (Avpro)

Wallop in Hampshire spent many months with a converted Skyship 600 airship, developing electronic equipment packages, operational mission profiles and the like for, reportedly, a counter-terrorism role in Northern Ireland. The villagers of Barton Stacey, Chilbolton and Stockbridge were unwitting witnesses to the development of a unique spy-in-the-sky which carried equipment from almost every leading British defence manufacturer. It would have stayed secret as well, but a US sub-contractor found it necessary to brag about its involvement.

Most of us, however, think of advanced, almost science-fiction designs, when we think of black programmes. We think of remotely-piloted aircraft or stealth bombers. In other words, complete platforms like the F-117 or B-2. Yet the reality is that 'black' is more associated with niche electronic programmes than complete platforms. Most of the United Kingdom's electronics companies regard the Farnborough-based Defence Evaluation & Research Agency (DERA) as the custodian of 'black' technology, theoretical and practical.

DERA, like the industry, talks little of black programmes, so detective work in this area can be difficult. Together with industry, including British Aerospace, GEC-Marconi and Rolls-Royce, DERA is working on programmes which will create the Future Offensive Air System (FOAS). This 20 to 25 year programme is designed to fulfil Staff Requirement (Air) 425 and was formerly known as Future Offensive Aircraft (FOA). Last year, research began to show that there was potential for it to be developed into concepts. Whether this technology demonstration vehicle is a wedge, bat-wing or double-delta we do not yet know.

The other possibility for FOAS is that it will be a large transport aircraft with a range of UCAVs and stand-off missiles. This is more unlikely because it is too radical for the air planners to take seriously, even if the Treasury think it is cheap.

The real future of black programmes is in the air space battle of the 2020-2035 period. To be safe in the prediction game is impossible, but here is a possible scenario that is not a million miles away from the views of the most senior people in the Royal Air Force — air defence of the UK in the third

Left: BAe's concept of a low-observable (LO) combat aircraft which may be the basis for a European 'black' combat aircraft programme. (BAe)

an uninhabited combat air vehicle (UCAV). Later this year, it is expected that France (Dassault) and Germany (Daimler-Benz Aerospace) will formally join the programme to create Europe's first real 'black' programme for combat aircraft.

Germany and France have developed space-based systems together and there have been other airframe programmes — Jaguar, Tornado and Eurofighter — but this will be the first truly revolutionary approach to air combat from the Europeans, since, well the eight-gun monoplane fighter in 1936. However, FOAS development may be a victim of the current UK Strategic Defence Review, as affordability is always the driver.

It may be cheaper in the long run to go for a UCAV but the technology is still high risk and proof will be needed before the defence chiefs go completely down that route. That is where the smaller companies in Europe come in — the avionics, flight control, communications and computer specialists. Certainly we can expect BAe and GEC to battle

with Lockheed-Martin for prime contractor integration but the enabling technologies will come from the companies past whose stands at the Farnborough Air Show many of us walk by without stopping to browse. Big mistake, for those companies have the technologies to create, for example, the synthetic environment needed to test concepts before metal or plastic is cut.

British Aerospace used the EAP programme to develop systems and reduce overall costs for the Eurofighter, therefore it is not too far from probability that BAe is now working on a technology demonstrator to prove FOAS

decade of the next century will be in the hands of the Eurofighter, tactical strike in a version of the Joint Strike Fighter and offensive strike will see the Tornado GR.4 phased out in favour of FOAS. FOAS will be a stealthy manned aircraft, conventionally-armed with cruise missiles and capable of acting as a mother for a series of specialist UCAVs — it will also be capable itself of being remotely-piloted from the ground or from another FOAS air vehicle. That concept will be pursued for reconnaissance and interdiction against enemy airfields. No more John Peters and John Nicole episodes, thank you!

Above: A Future Offensive Air System (FOAS) concept that could be produced in both manned and unmanned versions. (Avpro)

AFM Editor David Oliver looks into military aviation's crystal ball towards the day when the fighter pilot finally hangs up his 'g' suit.

SKY

S   k   8 9 0   y   r

FOR MANY MILITARY analysts, the future of military air power will put heavy emphasis on remotely-piloted aircraft, both the Unmanned Reconnaissance Aerial Vehicle (URAV) and, more controversially, the Unmanned Combat Aerial Vehicle (UCAV).

Neither are new concepts, as UCAVs were some of the first 'black' projects dating back to World War One. In Britain, H P Folland and Professor A M Low developed an 'aerial torpedo' in 1916. The small monoplane, built at the Royal Aircraft Establishment (RAE) at Farnborough under the cover name 'AT' (Aerial Target) had limited guidance and virtually no useful payload.

However, the breakthrough came when Americans Dr Peter Cooper and Elmer A Sperry invented the automatic gyroscopic stabiliser. With the aid of this technological breakthrough, they carried out limited tests with their first 'aerial torpedoes' at Long Island, New York,

in December 1917 using a converted US Navy Curtiss N-9 trainer powered by a 40hp engine and capable of carrying a 300lb (135kg) bomb load for 50 miles (80km).

A more sophisticated unmanned aircraft was designed by Charles F Kettering of Delco, later General

Motors. Powered by a 40hp Ford engine, the 12ft (3.6m) wingspan biplane, known as the 'Kettering Bug', could also carry a 300lb bomb load over short distances.

Launched from a trolley, the 'Bug' could be pre-programmed to drop on a target by an engine-driven cam

that would unscrew the wing retaining bolts over a set distance. The wings would then fold-up and the 'Bug' would dive vertically on to its target.

The unmanned 'flying bomb' concept was developed with very much more success into Germany's first secret weapon, the Fieseler Fi-103, better known as the V-1 'Revenge Weapon'. Project Kischkern (cherry-stone) was the code-name for the pulse-jet-powered aircraft carrying a 2,000lb (907kg) warhead designed to be launched from a 250ft (76m) long ramp, cruise at 400mph (645km/h) and be pre-programmed to fly between 100-150 miles (160-240km) before its engine cut out leaving it to drop on its target. Nearly 6,000 V-1s fell on British cities between June 1944 and January 1945, killing more than 900 people — mainly civilians.

The highly advanced V-1 was used to develop the United States' postwar missile and UAV programmes, the most successful of which was the Ryan Firebee family. Designed originally as an unmanned target drone, the Firebee was developed into a high- and low-altitude surveillance and electronic intelligence (ELINT) UAV during the Vietnam War under the code-name Lightning Bug .

Under another 'black' programme of the mid-1970s, the Firebee became the first UCAV when it dropped bombs and launched missiles. Trials were carried out with an armed version of the Firebee, known as Pathfinder, fitted with laser designator and low-light TV cameras in the nose used to acquire targets for a variety of air-to-ground weapons ranging from Mk 82 iron bombs to Maverick air-to-ground missiles. Guided by operators in the its 'mother' launch plane, a DC-130, the Firebees were not only able to find their targets but they could also hit them with some accuracy. However, the end of the war in Vietnam also spelt the end of the Firebee bomber.

Other 'black' unmanned programmes that were spawned by the South East Asia conflicts was the Mach 3 D-21 *Tagboard* (see page 18) which suffered from being in front of the then known technology, and the ultra secret Teledyne Ryan Model 154 Compass Arrow. This was the first high-altitude reconnaissance UAV to have contoured structural shapes that shadowed engine intakes and exhaust ducts with radiation absorbing to minimise its radar cross-section. Stealth had been discovered but it would be another 20 years before stealthy UAVs were back in fashion.

Although small piston-engined model aircraft-like UAVs had been built by Israel and acquired by US forces for use during the Gulf War, it was the Defense Advanced Research Projects Agency's (DARPA) Tier project that introduced a new generation of UAVs that would push known technologies to their practical limits.

The first of the USAF's 'dream team'

Above: *The Dark-Star, a stealthy Unmanned Reconnaissance Aerial Vehicle (URAV) destined for the USAF's 11th Reconnaissance Squadron. (Lockheed Martin/Boeing)*

Left: *The Avpro Archangel Unmanned Combat Aerial Vehicle (UCAV) concept is being offered to DERA as a Future Offensive Air System (FOAS) option. (Avpro)*

of high-tech UAVs was the General Dynamics' Predator developed from a CIA 'black' programme, the Gnat 750. Officially known as the Tier II Medium-Altitude Endurance (MAE) UAV, Predator first flew in June 1995 and a year later was flown operationally over Bosnia by the USAF's 11th Reconnaissance Squadron (RS) based at Indian Springs AFAF— part of the Nellis AFB complex in the Nevada Desert — in support of IFOR.

Although Predator is a conventional design built largely of composite materials and powered by a 44hp pusher piston engine, it has an endurance of 40 hours at a cruising altitude of 25,000ft (7,620m) carrying a 450lb (204kg) sensor payload. Its larger cousin, the Teledyne Ryan Global Hawk, or Tier II Plus High-Altitude Endurance (HAE) surveillance UAV, is powered by a 'low burn' 7,050lb st Rolls-Royce Allison turbofan. The performance of this large UAV, it has a wingspan of 116ft (35.5m), is impressive. It can remain airborne for more than 40 hours, cruise at 375mph (603km/h) at 65,000ft (1,980m) and has a maximum range of 14,500 miles (23,335km). Its 2,000lb (908kg) payload comprises Electro Optical (EO), Infra-Red (IR), Synthetic Aperture Radar (SAR) sensors, active and passive Electronic Support Measures (ESM), on-board data storage and real-time transmission.

The third, and most unconventional of the three Tier project UAVs is the Lockheed Martin/Boeing DarkStar. Tier III Minus is a medium-size Williams FJ-44 turbofan-powered stealthy surveillance UAV designed to loiter unseen over a battlefield for up to eight hours. A product of the Skunk Works, DarkStar first flew in March 1996, but due to a software

problem the prototype crashed on its second flight a month later. A second DarkStar is scheduled to fly in March this year.

All three production Tier URAVs will be operated by the 11th RS at Indian Springs, although some systems will be assigned to overseas Detachments in the same way as the 99th RW operates its fleet of manned U-2s (see page 58).

The next, and more controversial step in UAV development is the UCAV. Many countries, and the United States in particular, find the loss of operational aircrew in the 'bush' wars and internal conflicts that have broken out all over the world since the end of the Cold War, unacceptable. Therefore the UCAV is seen as the ideal solution to perform 'dull, dirty and dangerous' missions. In an age of declining defence budgets, increasing requirements and the continuing development of technology, the UCAV could be an ideal and cost-effective force multiplier. The UCAV would have long endurance and high manoeuvrability beyond human endurance, high sortie rates, low radar signature and excellent survivability. Obvious roles for the UCAV are suppression of enemy defences (SEAD), covert reconnaissance/strike, fixed target attack, support jamming and bomb damage assessment (BDA). Further down the line are cruise missile defence, defensive and offensive counter-air and combat rescue.

Although acquisition, training and operations should be significantly lower in cost than manned aircraft,

Above Right: Two 20ft (6m) long low-observable (LO) UCAVs strike an enemy airfield with highly accurate penetrating weapons. (Lockheed Martin)

Right: A UK design for an unmanned naval strike vehicle from Avpro, which would also launch and recover vertically from an advanced assault ship. (Avpro)

some argue that the doctrine of how, where, when and why UCAVs should be used will be the determining factor of their development. There are also a number of technical problems to be overcome before UCAVs replace the manned fighter. As they will not have to be flown regularly for pilot continuation training, UCAVs will have to be stored for most of their in-service life. This means that these highly sophisticated vehicles will have to be ready to go into action at a few hours notice. Their avionics systems and sensors will have to remain alert even when stored. A new breed of engine that will not require long-term preservative materials has to be developed, as must small size and lightweight weapon systems that can be available at potential trouble spots where UCAVs need to be deployed. Formulas to integrate UCAVs with manned combat must be fail-safe if deconfliction or even accidental shoot-downs are to be avoided. This would be absolutely vital during such multi-national operations such as the Gulf War or Bosnia, and ground targets would have to be positively identified before any UCAV attack.

New ways of protecting secure UCAV data-links from being jammed or distorted will have to be addressed and they may have to be fitted with self-destruct systems in the event of loss of operator control or disruption of its autonomous pre-programmed mission.

The prospect of 'rogue' UCAVs dropping their weapons on 'friendly' forces, being damaged by enemy action or simply crashing out of control and creating civilian casualties, would seriously curtail UCAV acceptance. They would have to be more reliable than current commercial aircraft if they are to gain the confidence of operators. Yet more challenges for the UCAV designer...

One area where the UCAV could be particularly effective is when operating with maritime forces. Apart from launching and recovering UCAVs from conventional aircraft carriers and warship helipads, a return of small aviation support vessels designed to carry a small but lethal URAV/UCAV force could make them a practical proposition for many smaller navies. Maritime targets can be easily identified and attacked by

unmanned vehicles, and the aforementioned dangers of UCAV 'accidents' would be minimised during over-sea operations. Even submarines could carry small numbers of specially adapted URAV/UCAVs which could be launched from under the surface, in much the same way as Polaris missiles.

It is obvious that only a few countries will have the technological and economic resources to be able to develop and operate practical UCAVs in the foreseeable future and it will come as no surprise to find that the United States is leading the race. Most of its top aerospace companies are submitting UCAV concepts to DARPA, while the US services are struggling to grasp their potential. At present, the US Navy has no validated missions or official requirements for these systems, although the US Marine Corps is close to having some. The USAF is looking forward to building its operational UAV experience when Global Hawk and DarkStar join Predator with the 11th Reconnaissance Squadron, and is actively studying how UCAVs can be integrated with its future F-22 and JSF fleets.

The United Kingdom is beginning to put UCAVs in the frame for the Future Offensive Air System (FOAS) which will replace the RAF Tornado GR.1/GR.4 force. Subject to the findings of the latest government Defence Review, one FOAS option gaining serious consideration by military planners is for a mixed force of manned aircraft and UCAVs.

However, both the USA and UK agree that the deployment of the first combat 'sky robots' will not be before the year 2020!

Above: *A Lockheed Martin concept of a vertical take-off and landing unmanned naval strike vehicle to be launched and recovered from an advanced assault ship.*

Left: *A small stealthy UCAV with folding wings which would enable it to be carried on submarines and launched beneath the surface. (Photos Lockheed Martin)*

BLACK SURVIVORS

Preserved Black Aircraft
Compiled by Mark Nicholls

Below: SR-71A 64-17960 forms part of the Castle Air Museum collection at Atwater, California, and along with the rest of the exhibits is beautifully presented in landscaped surroundings. (AFM - Dave Allport)

D ESPITE THE HIGHLY classified nature of these aircraft and their mission profiles during the early part of their careers, time has allowed them to emerge from the darkness. In spite of changes in policy and the introduction of new technology these aircraft are still of a special breed and consequently very valuable. On the first retirement of the SR-71A Blackbird not a single aircraft was scrapped, instead many were presented to museums, while a small number were kept in storage at the Lockheed Martin Skunk Works at Palmdale, California — which turned out to be a good decision. We are indeed fortunate that so many examples of these revolutionary designs are now publicly available allowing us to marvel at the extraordinary appearance and capabilities of these 'black' aircraft.

Right: Basking under the hot Arizona sunshine is SR-71A 64-17951 at the magnificent Pima Air and Space Museum, Tucson, Arizona. (Mark Nicholls)

Below: The distinctive slender shape of the Blackbird is shown to good effect in this study of SR-71A 64-17973 at the Blackbird Airpark, Palmdale, California. (AFM -Duncan Cubitt)

Above: *Currently in store at Edwards AFB, California, is SR-71A 64-17955, part of the extensive Air Force Flight Test Center Museum which is located there. (AFM - Steve Fletcher)*

Left: *A-12 60-6931 belongs to the Minnesota Air National Guard Historical Museum, Minneapolis, Minnesota, and is arguably one of the best examples of the A-12 to be found. (AFM - Duncan Cubitt)*

Left: *Long-time home for the SR-71A Blackbird during its operational career was Beale AFB, California — so fittingly this aircraft, 64-17963, is preserved beside the ramp together with a GDT-21B drone. (AFM - Alan Warnes)*

Type	Serial	Location
A-12	60-6924	Blackbird Airpark, Palmdale, California
A-12	60-6925	Intrepid Air-Sea-Space Museum, New York
A-12	60-6927	Lockheed Martin, Plant 42, Palmdale, California (stored)
A-12	60-6930	US Space and Rocket Center, Huntsville, Alabama
A-12	60-6931	Minnesota Air National Guard Historical Museum, Minneapolis, Minnesota
A-12	60-6933	San Diego Aerospace Museum, Balboa Park, San Diego, California
YF-12A	60-6935	USAF Museum, Wright-Patterson AFB, Ohio
A-12	60-6937	Lockheed Martin, Plant 42, Palmdale, California
A-12	60-6938	USS Alabama Battleship Commission, Mobile, Alabama
A-12	60-6940	Museum of Flight, Seattle, Washington
YF-117A	79-10780	Nellis AFB, Nevada
YF-117A	79-10781	USAF Museum, Wright-Patterson AFB, Ohio
F-117A	80-0785	Lockheed Martin, Plant 42, Palmdale, California
SR-71A	64-17951	Pima Air and Space Museum. Tucson, Arizona
SR-71A	64-17955	Air Force Flight Test Center Museum, Edwards AFB, California (stored)
SR-71A	64-17958	Museum of Aviation, Robins AFB, Georgia
SR-71A	64-17959	USAF Armament Museum, Eglin AFB, Florida
SR-71A	64-17960	Castle Air Museum, Atwater, California
SR-71A	64-17961	Kansas Cosmosphere and Space Center, Hutchinson, Kansas
SR-71A	64-17963	Beale AFB, California
SR-71A	64-17964	SAC Museum, Mahonie State Park, Nebraska
SR-71A	64-17972	NASM, Washington, DC (stored)
SR-71A	64-17973	Blackbird Airpark, Palmdale, California
SR-71A	64-17975	March AFB Museum, Riverside, California
SR-71A	64-17976	USAF Museum, Wright-Patterson AFB, Ohio
SR-71A	64-17979	USAF History and Traditions Museum, Lackland AFB, Texas
SR-71C	64-17981	Hill Aerospace Museum, Utah
U-2A	56-6722	USAF Museum, Wright-Patterson AFB, Ohio
U-2C	56-6680	NASM, Washington, DC
U-2C	56-6681	NASA Ames Research Center, Moffett Field, California
U-2C	56-6682	Museum of Aviation, Robins AFB, Georgia
U-2C	56-6691 (3512)	Military Museum, Beijing, China (wreckage, Taiwanese markings)
U-2C	56-6692	Imperial War Museum, Duxford, UK
U-2C	56-6693	Central Museum of the Armed Forces, Moscow, Russia (remains of Gary Powers' aircraft)
U-2C	56-6701	SAC Museum, Mahonie State Park, Nebraska
U-2C	56-6707	Laughlin AFB, Texas
U-2C	56-6714	Beale AFB, California
U-2C	56-6716	Warrior Park, Davis-Monthan AFB, Arizona
U-2D	56-6721	Lockheed Martin, Plant 42, Palmdale, California
U-2CT	56-6953	Bodø, Norway

Wreckage from three other U-2s shot down while operating in Taiwanese markings over China is known to exist but the exact where-abouts and identities of these aircraft is unknown.

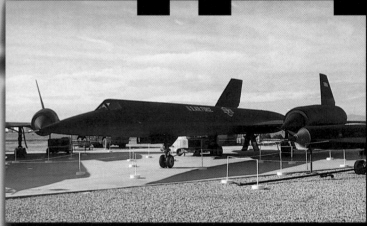

The home of the Lockheed Skunk Works and birth place of many of these unique aircraft is Palmdale, California, and a small area called the Blackbird Airpark has been set up beside the turning to the airport terminal. On display are an A-12, SR-71A and a D-21 drone, together with several pieces of support equipment. (AFM - Duncan Cubitt)

Now on show in the recently opened American Air Museum at the Imperial War Museum, Duxford, is U-2C 56-6692. Suspended above the giant B-52D the aircraft strikes a dramatic pose. This aircraft was donated by the USAF after having served as an instructional trainer at RAF Alconbury during the late 1980s. (AFM - Duncan Cubitt)

Beautifully presented U-2C 56-6707 is to be found at Laughlin AFB, Texas, from where these aircraft operated early on in their USAF career. (AFM - Alan Warnes)

Dramatically mounted among the base buildings at Beale AFB, California, is U-2C 56-6714. The base has been synonymous with the Dragon Lady for many years and is the current home to the 9th Reconnaissance Wing fleet of U-2R/S aircraft. (AFM - Alan Warnes)

Left: Probably the most spectacularly displayed example of any 'black aircraft' is A-12 60-6933 at the San Diego Aerospace Museum in Balboa Park, San Diego, California. The entrance to the museum building is to the left of the aircraft which requires three poles to keep it aloft. (AFM Dave Allport)

Left: SR-71A 64-17975 is now part of the March AFB Museum collection at Riverside, California, and still wears Det 1 markings on its tail fins. (AFM - Dave Allport)

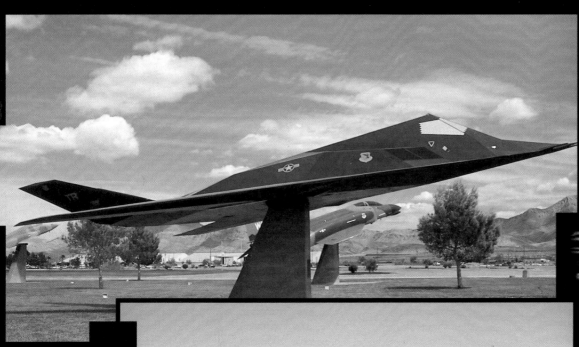

Left: Only three Stealth Fighters are presently preserved in the US but easily the most impressive is YF-117A 79-10780, the first pre-production aircraft, which can be found at Nellis AFB, Nevada. (AFM - Steve Fletcher)

Left: The Warrior Park at Davis-Monthan AFB, Arizona, is now home to U-2C 56-6716, part of a small collection dispersed among the shrubbery and palm trees. (AFM - Dave Allport)

Bottom left: The Strategic Air Command Museum at Offutt AFB, Nebraska is being relocated to Mahonie State Park some 25 miles away, but captured here while still on display at Offutt is U-2C 56-6701. The museum's SR-71A 64-17964 has already been moved and is now displayed in the entrance hall at the new site. (AFM - Duncan Cubitt)

Right: *NASA's Blackbird N844NA (ex - USAF 64-17980) making its first flight with the X-33 Linear Aerospike SR-71 Experiment (LASRE) power-plant from the Dryden Flight Research Center at Edwards AFB on October 31, 1997. (NASA)*

Below: *The last of the breed. NASA's two-seat SR-71B N831NA (ex-USAF 64-17956) is one of only two Mach 3 test platforms available in the foreseeable future. (NASA)*

FLY
NASA
n a s a

HAVING PEAKED DURING the manned moon landings of the 1970s, America's National Aeronautics and Space Administration (NASA) came down to earth, both with its budgets, and its projects, in subsequent years.

Now there is a resurgence of 'space' programmes ranging from Hyper-X, (see page 53) to the X-33 VentureStar (see page 3), and high-speed, high-altitude flight trials for these projects are carried out by 30-year old SR-71 Blackbirds.

Between 1969 and 1979, two Mach 3 YF-12 aircraft were used in a joint NASA/USAF programme, and since 1990 NASA crews from the Dryden Flight Research Facility at Edwards AFB have flown two SR-71s on loan from the USAF for training and scientific research flights, and kept a third in storage. NASA also operates a variant of the U-2 'spyplane' — two ER-2s, for a variety of test programmes and environmental monitoring.

NASA originally operated three U-2C aircraft which were replaced by modified TR-1As when the U-2R line was re-opened. Other U-2s have been loaned to NASA by the USAF.

Above: *NASA's ER-2 N708NA/80-1097 configured to carry a Senior Span-type dorsal fairing known as Starlink, has recently moved from the Ames Research Center at NAS Moffett Field to Dryden at Edwards AFB. (AFM-David Oliver)*